What Really Killed Rosebud?

Robert Christiansen Jr.
TRUE CRIME

WHAT REALLY KILLED ROSEBUD?

BY CLAIRE BURCH

REGENT PRESS
BERKELEY
2001

Library of Congress Cataloging-in-Publication Data

Burch, Claire
    What really killed rosebud? by Claire Burch.
        p. cm.
    ISBN 0-916147-69-X
    1. Homicide--California--Berkeley--Case studies. 2. Denovo,
Rosebud. 3. Riots--California--Berkeley. 4. Parks--California--
Berkeley. I. Title.

HV6534.B44 B87 2000
322.4'092
[B]   00-030627

Manufactured in the U.S.A.

REGENT PRESS
6020-A Adeline
Oakland, CA 94608
regent@sirius.com

ontents

1977, Age 3

1977, Age 4

1979, Age 5

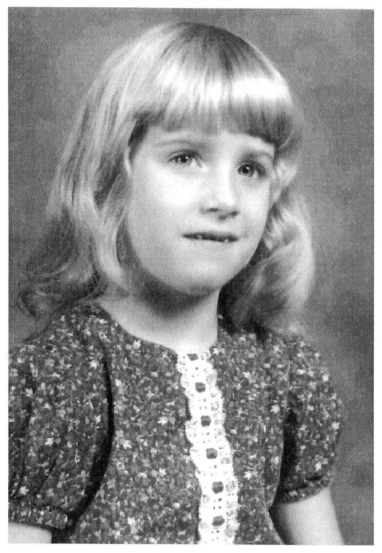

1979, Age 6

1980, Age 7

1982, Age 9

1984, Age 10

1985, Age 11

1987, Age 14

1988, Age 14

1989, Age 15

1990, Age 17

1992, Age 19

Contrasting Views Of UC Intruder

By Yuml Wilson and Peter Fimrite
Chronicle Staff Writers

Depending on who you talk to, the 19-year old woman who was fatally shot yesterday after breaking into the UC Berkeley chancellor's home with a machete was either a revolutionary heroine or a crazy person.

There is little doubt that Rosebud Abigail Denovo, who was born as Laura Miller, believed passionately in her cause and was willing to use illegal and violent means. But the question that may never be answered is, "Why?"

"I knew she was not crazy — she was righteously angry," said Gina Sasso, 30, a member of the People's Park Defense Union and a candidate for the Berkeley City Council. "She was sometimes foolish and impulsive. She was very committed and very smart. It's a horrible waste."

A different picture comes from an Alameda County probation report prepared after her arrest last year for possessing illegal explosives at a Berkeley hillside campsite.

Denovo had a history of causing trouble that began at age 5 in her hometown of Lexington, Ky., the report said. By age 12, she was described as angry and rebellious, often running away and fighting constantly with her schoolmates. According to the report, she once threatened to kill her middle-school principal.

Some called her a brilliant revolutionary; others called her crazy

A behavior disorder was diagnosed in Denovo when she was 14, the report said. According to one news account, she was hospitalized in a psychiatric hospital in Lexington from September 1987 to June 1986.

She was also described as "extremely brilliant" by sources quoted in the report, passing her high school equivalency exam at the end of her junior year. A friend said she spent a year at Moore-head State University in Kentucky before heading west.

The San Francisco Chronicle

She changed her name to Rosebud Abigail Denovo so her initials would spell "RAD," according to the probation report.

During the past two years, Denovo has been arrested or questioned at least a dozen times by university police for prowling and weapons charges, said university spokeswoman Gretchen Kell.

She had been free on bail pending a September 14 trial in Alameda County Superior Court on charges of possessing explosives after her arrest Aug. 8, 1991, at a homeless encampment east of UC Berkeley's Clark Kerr Campus.

She and her boyfriend at the time, Andrew James Barnum, 31, had been linked to the discovery at the campsite of home made explosives, a marked campus map and a list of university employees.

Police also confiscated a diary that indicated that Denovo had planned to bomb Berkeley City Hall and the chancellor's home as part of a scheme to overthrow the U.S. government.

The diary said the bombings would rally a "national people's army to destroy the means of oppression" and discussed a plan called COUGAR: Conspiracy to Overthrow Unlawfully the Government of Amerikka by Revolutions-. The plan included blowing up the U.S. Capitol building and hijacking and detonating an MX missile.

An entry dated June 25, 1991, read: "Tien, you're not getting off that easy. Man, I want to destroy something."

Denovo and Barnum had been heavily involved at People's Park, where protesters unsuccessfully tried to block construction of the volleyball courts. Denovo was arrested in People's Park on July 3 for battery on a police officer during a demonstration and again on July 31 for trespassing and prowling near the Doe Library.

Denovo struggled with authority since childhood

By Susan Stern
Tribune staff writer

Just a month before Berkeley radical Rosebud Denovo was killed while brandishing a machete in the UC-Berkeley chancellor's home, she told her father she might enroll at UC Berkeley.

Denovo's father and mother, Green and Carolyn Miller, were visiting from Kentucky in what Denovo's friends called a reconciliation after a tumultuous childhood.

"At the time, we felt very, very good," Green Miller said yesterday. "We felt things were finally going in the fight direction."

But progress went awry Tuesday morning, when Denovo broke into the chancellor's home and was shot to death by police.

Denovo, who had taken up the People's Park cause, was arrested last year with explosives meant to blow up the chancellor's home. Tuesday, she bore a note: "We are willing to die for this Property," it said. "Are you?"

Several seemingly contradic-tory desires — such as wanting to kill Chancellor 'Chang-Lin Tien and enroll in his school — emerged yesterday as mental health professionals, Berkeley politicos and Denovo's family tried to make sense of the tragedy.

According to an Alameda County probation report, Denovo had first seen a therapist at the age of 5, and was committed to a mental hospital twice, at ages 14 and 18.

She had hit a friend, threatened the life of the vice principal of her middle school and run away from home. But according to the report, she was never diagnosed as psychotic. Her diagnoses ranged from "personality disorder" to "conduct disorder" to "obsessive/compulsive traits."

San Francisco psychiatrist Dr. Lenore Terr said that Denovo was still sick. "Most of the people in our society who do violence are not psychotic," said Terr, an expert in childhood trauma. "The kind of diagnosis

Denovo _____

Continued from Page A-3

she had perfectly fits the kind of person who ends up in someone's house with a machete."

But Berkeley psychiatrist Dr. Neal Blumfeld said Denovo's troubles were only half the problem. He said she appears to have been someone who was extremely sensitive to injustice, who was stressed by the country's rightward tilt and economic decline. "Governor Wilson doesn't seem to care if there's a budget and Bush doesn't admit there's economic problems in the country. The authority figures are cruel. The university wants to bulldoze People's Park. I imagine to someone who is not jaded, this could really stir them up."

David Beauvais, Denovo's attorney, argued yesterday that her acts were consistent with her anarchist writings and work in the anti-war, civil rights and homeless movements. Her attempted attack on Tien was not mental illness, but political martyrdom, he said.

"She was the kind of a person who was willing to put her body and soul on the line for what she believed in," Beauvais said. "In 50 years it's conceivable she'll be in high school textbooks of American history as a freedom fighter of the past."

Yet Terr argued that Denovo's political ideas and her writings threatening the president and the pope, were less significant than her threats against the vice principal and the chancellor.

"Before she'd even heard of People's Park, she had it in for the vice principal," Terr said. "There's a pattern in this girl's life. A problem with educational authorities."

Which leads to the question of whether the problem started at home. Denovo's father, Green Miller, is dean of the economics department at Moorehead State University in Kentucky.

He said yesterday that he couldn't understand why his daughter harbored such strong anti-authority feelings.

Even though the Millers committed their daughter to the mental hospital after years of family discord, Miller said yesterday his daughter was "someone who loved us," and "brought happiness to our homes."

Terr said there is no way to know without more information whether Denovo's anti-authority attitude started at home.

—Staff writer Tracie Reynolds contributed to this report.

Activists question campus shooting

They wonder why police didn't just surround UC chancellor's home, wait out intruder

By Erin McCormick
SPECIAL TO THE EXAMINER

BERKELEY — The question gnaws at activists, her friends and a member of the Berkeley police commission:

If Rosebud Denovo's intended victims were out of the house and she no longer posed an immediate threat to anyone, why didn't police simply surround the UC-Berkeley chancellor's mansion and attempt to negotiate her surrender?

Instead, the machete-wielding Denovo was confronted Tuesday morning in an upstairs bedroom, police said. And it was there that she was shot in the heart by an Oakland police officer who had recently returned to duty after having been shot five times himself by a robbery suspect.

Officer Craig Chew, 26, fired after Denovo — a troubled 20-year old with a history of run-ins with the law — lunged at him, UC Berkeley Police Lt. Patrick Carroll said.

UC-Berkeley police were in charge of the situation that includ-ed officers from the Oakland and Berkeley city police departments. Bob Sanders, a university spokesman, said police would not comment on the tactical decision made on Tuesday because it may jeopardize their investigation of the shooting.

But Berkeley Police Review Commissioner Osha Neumann questioned why police commanders ever let Officer Chew get into such a dangerous and potentially violent situation.

Neumann's commission has no purview over university police operations, and UC has no such commission of its own. Still, Neumann wonders why, once Chancellor Chang-Lin Tien and his wife, Di Hwa, were escorted out of the house by police, officers could not have taken the time to develop a plan to coax or flush Denovo out of the building.

The Tiens' exit "should have provided police time to develop a strategy to minimize the risk to the officer and also the suspect," Neumann said. "Having an officer, presumably with his gun drawn, enter rooms where he doesn't know what's inside is the most risky scenario I can imagine."

UC-Berkeley police declined to provide a copy of their policy on dealing With barricaded suspects, saying its release would compromise security. But a 1988 Berkeley city police policy emphasizes two goals: protecting the lives of everybody involved, including the suspect, and taking the time necessary to resolve crises without injuries.

"As much time as may be necessary will be used to ensure the nonviolent resolution of such situations even if a number of days is required," states the policy, which reflects standard police proce-

From *The San Francisco Examiner,* August 27, 1992. (Reprinted With Permission.)

dures. Berkeley Lt. Tom Grant said, however, that "There are so many things that happen that require an officer's discretion, it's hard to say there's a set policy."

Friends and activists who knew Denovo — a homeless People's Park activist — are calling for an independent investigation of the police handling of the situation.

"It didn't have to go down this way," said Denovo's attorney, David Beauvais. "There were 1,000 different ways the police could have handled this without killing her."

Questions about the police tactics have fueled the anger among protesters who demonstrated with Denovo over university construction of volleyball courts at People's Park.

"Where are the rubber bullets when we need them?" said activist Aaron Handel. "In this case there was no Mace, no tear gas, just bullets to the chest. Why didn't they flush her out with gas?"

The incident began at 5:51 a.m. Tuesday, when Denovo tripped a silent alarm as she used a blowtorch to break into the north campus mansion where the chancellor and his wife slept, Carroll said.

Oakland K-9 units were called in to search the building and, after the first floor was checked, the Tiens, were safely removed from the house.

Police continued to search the three-story mansion for Denovo and a police dog detected her in a second-floor bedroom.

University spokesman Sanders said that as Chew tried to open the bedroom door through a connecting bathroom, Denovo swung the door open, pushing the officer backward into a bathtub.

Then, Carroll said, Denovo lunged at the prone officer with the machete raised in her hands.

Chew fired three times, hitting Denovo once where her hands gripped the machete and twice in the chest, Carroll said.

The shooting brought together two people with tragic histories.

Denovo had a long police record, including an arrest for possession of explosives, and a history of psychiatric problems.

Chew, a three-year veteran of the Oakland Police Department had returned to full-time duty last month, after being shot five times by a robbery suspect a year ago, according to Oakland Police Capt. Jim Hahn.

After a North Oakland robbery, Chew was approaching a parked car when a 15-year-old suspect standing near it suddenly fired on him, wounding him critically in the chest. Chew returned fire, wounding the suspect in the leg.

Prior to joining the Oakland force, Chew spent two years as a Berkeley officer. During that time, the city manager upheld three police review commission complaints against him, including one for excessive force.

In that complaint, according to, Berkeley Commission Review records, a man he arrested during a brawl at a university dance claimed the officer kicked him in the groin and jabbed him with a baton without any physical provocation.

The city does not disclose whether officers are disciplined after complaints are upheld, saying it's a private personnel matter.

However, even some friends of Denovo's believe she knew what she was getting into when she broke into the chancellor's house, and got exactly what she wanted: a dramatic, early death.

"Rosebud," said People's Park activist Michael Delacour, "probably wanted to go down in a big way.

Obsession with park cited in UC death

Denovo's friends say her attack was for the People's Park cause

By Erin McCormick
SPECIAL TO THE EXAMINER

BERKELEY — The ragtag piece of university land known as People's Park hardly looks like a cause worth dying for.

For more than 20 years the park's overgrown thickets and bald patches of grass have been a haven for the disenfranchised and a seemingly unending source of political controversy.

But Tuesday, 20-year old activist Rosebud Denovo took the tensions surrounding the park to a new height when she broke into the UC Berkeley chancellor's mansion wielding a machete, on what some say may have been a suicide mission to avenge the university's handling of the park.

To Denovo and other activists, the park represented much more than just a one-square-block recreational area.

Since 1969, when Vietnam War protesters moved in to take over the piece of vacant land and turn it into a park, it has been held up as a symbol of the liberal ideals of the 60s — a symbol Denovo apparently thought was worth her own life.

According to friends, Denovo saw the park as a testing ground for her anarchistic take on self-government and as a monument to the tenets of free speech.

"She would have said that People's Park represented the concept of liberated space, where people could do what they wanted and be free of concepts like liability insurance and police," said activist Dave Lind, a close friend of Denovo's.

So Denovo and other activists were enraged by any university attempt to assert authority over the land.

Many park supporters shared Denovo's anger at the university's recent construction of volleyball courts and other amenities.

Most say they never expected her to act on it in a way that would end with her being shot in the heart by police while invading the chancellor's mansion. In her duffel bag that day was a note calling for the removal of all university developments in the park.

"Whatever Rosebud had in mind, she didn't tell anybody,

People's Park
continued from Page A-3

because they would have stopped her," said Doug Horngrad, the attorney for De-novo's longtime boyfriend, Andrew Barnum. "Clearly, this was something going on in her own head."

Police records portray Denovo as a disturbed young woman with a long list of arrests, who allegedly collected materials to build bombs and wrote of her desires to kill the chancellor and overthrow the government.

Activists remember the homeless runaway as a soft-spoken and virtually fearless woman, who always stayed on the sidelines of organizing meetings.

Once demonstrations started, however, she was part of the "action faction," which favored a more confrontational approach dealing with police, according to Lind.

"She could be pretty provocative," he said. "She would burn flags, and when the cops attacked, she would fight back."

Another friend said Denovo at times had established a home base under a bush in the park. And, though she had no home and so little money that "she lived on Pepsi and candy bars," Lind said, she was tireless in organizing efforts to raise funds to bail out arrested protesters.

"This movement was her life — she lived it and breathed it," he said. "Obviously, she was prepared to die for it, if on a small scale it would wake people up."

Indeed, the incident has reignited protests in the park. The scene there had just begun to quiet down after a tumultuous year of demonstrations beginning with last August's riots over the university's construction of volleyball courts.

The university and City of Berkeley recently completed a series of yearlong construction projects designed to clean up the park, but activists vowed their fight against the new sports courts would continue.

"We're still in the middle of a war here," said activist Eli Yates.

Milton Fujii, the university's director of community affairs, said he believed Denovo's actions had more to do with her desire to lash out at authority than with the park.

"I think the fact that she was here at this place at this time was a coincidence of history," he said. "It could have easily been a nuclear power plant or the Pentagon or almost any symbol of authority that she picked to lash out at.

"All we want is for it to be a place where everyone can feel comfortable and enjoy themselves in the outdoors."

Oakland ☀ Tribune

A PULITZER PRIZE - WINNING NEWSPAPER

OAKLAND, CALIFORNIA | COUNTY EDITION | WEDNESDAY, AUGUST 26, 1992

PEOPLE'S PARK ACTIVIST SHOT TO DEATH INSIDE UC CHANCELLOR'S RESIDENCE

Rosebud Abigail Denovo, 20, shown here at a February 1991 protest at Berkeley's Sproul Plaza, has a history of radical activism and brushes with the law.

Her life marched to a different drum

By Kevin Fagan and Paul Grabowicz
Tribune staff writers

From the day she ran away from home at age 12 until she was killed by a policeman's bullet yesterday, two weeks after her 20th birthday, Rosebud Abigail Denovo was filled with an angry passion to crush out authority.

As a youngster she threatened to kill the vice principal of her middle school in Lexington, Ky., and fought bitterly with her parents and any student who she thought slighted her.

As a young woman she was arrested on suspicion of building bombs to use against University of California officials, and penned poetry about killing the president and the pope. She wrote obsessively in her diaries of sparking a revolution, and of planting a bomb in the UC chancellor's house.

Whether that was her intent yester-day when she broke into Chancellor Chang Lin-Tien's house with a machete and a hunting knife is a secret she took to her grave. An officer shot her as she lunged toward him in a second-story bathroom.

The only clue she left was a note in a duffel bag saying she wanted authorities to stop "interfering" with People's Park in Berkeley, and that she was "willing to die for the land."

And the only legacy she left was the memory of a fiery and often angry homeless protester, hailed as brilliant and sweet by her friends and branded by police as deranged and a constant irritant.

A petite woman at 5 feet 1 inch and 105 pounds, she left an indelible impression on all she met.

In the spirit of Rosebud

Demonstrators show anger in street action after the killing: She would have wanted it that way

The evening of Rosebud Denovo's death about 150 people gathered in People's Park. Many rumors had been in the air all day about the killing of Rosebud with many different perspectives on the tragedy, but there was a general consensus that the police didn't have to kill Rosebud. Many emotions were flowing from shock to sadness to rage.

A few UC Bureaucrats, including UC PR person Milton Fuji, showed up and sparked an angry reaction from people gathered. Many people got in their faces and told them to "get the fuck outta here" and as Fuji was leaving he got hit in the back with a cardboard garbage can. Fuji, being a good UC stooge, later wrote an incredibly propagandistic column printed in the Oakland Tribune and the Daily Cal, that People's Park activists were a racist lynch mob. Many people responded with letters and columns to Fuji's utter bullshit.

A little while later a short march to the UC police station of about 200 people happened with people chanting and shouting in grief and rage. The scene was tense but eventually people filtered away to later regather at the park.

People gathered in the Park at 9 p.m. with lots of cops and media lurking around. Many homeless people and street youth, who generally don't come to protests, showed up in full force and were visibly upset about Rosebud's murder. Many people urged revenge, while others argued against it. During the angry discussion an individual started to saw on the volleyball courts, prompting many others to start doing damage to the courts. The police moved in, clubbing several people and the response for many was to go hand to hand with the cops.

A tense atmosphere had erupted. Cops knocked one person unconscious and protesters responded with some rock throwing. Several arrests were made including John Vance and Andy Barnum (Rosebud's boyfriend). Barnum is still in jail.

A few minutes later a bonfire broke out on the corner of Telegraph and Haste and a crowd of about 150 people gathered. At this point the cops laid back. Down Haste people started ripping down construction wood from the new UC dorm at 2424 Channing and a large barricade was built and set on fire. Many people began throwing rocks at the police. Many people joined in and the crowd was openly defiant and noticeably diverse including homeless, youth, activists, people of color, students and women.

As police formed skirmish lines they moved toward the crowd attempting to disperse it. The crowd broke down into smaller, mobile groups. Protesters moved around the Southside running from police charges, setting bonfires in several intersections, making barricades, attempting to overturn a police car and smashing at least two others. At different points in the night people openly chased police away making for a angry celebration.

At one point in the night people began inflicting damage on a UC construction site on Durant near Shattuck. Police finally scattered the rioters using vehicles and officers on foot in tandem. A number of arrests occurred throughout the night.

People's anger was extremely focused against the police and the UC. No looting occurred despite the generic claims of the media who portrayed the night as just "Another Riot in Berkeley." The riot was both unified and militant and did have a real sense of purpose even if the purpose was to do some damage. People felt powerful.

Though there was sense of wanting to avenge Rosebud's killing and many people felt Rosebud would have wanted us to riot, the rebellion went deeper than a police killing or People's Park or hatred of the police and UC. It was about daily anger and frustration and trying to reclaim some spirit against the alienation, misery, and repression of this rotten system that denies human potential and its ability to create something better.

THE LADY IN THE LAVATORY

BY MICHAEL MECHANIC

As parents of UC Berkeley's new freshman class drove into town to deliver their children to the threshold of adulthood, they were welcomed by boarded-up windows, cops in riot gear, and news of a troubled young woman's death at the hands of the police. Early the previous morning, in the elegant campus home of UC Berkeley chancellor Chang-Lin Tien, shots rang out from in upstairs bathroom. Oakland Police Officer Craig Chew brought the life of nineteen-year-old People's Park activist Rosebud Abigail Denovo to a premature end.

The shots resounded across the nation. Here in town, street vendors quickly upped their supplies of "Fuck the Police!" T-shirts. Campus administrators called for beefed-up security. Cops braced for the protests and rioting that were sure to follow. "Machete-wielding Woman Slain," announced headlines coast-to-coast. Had the headlines been written by Denovo's activist friends, people sitting down to breakfast in her home state of Kentucky might have read: "'Brave Teen Anarchist Murdered by Pigs.'"

Only a police officer and a dead woman know the truth of what happened in that upstairs room. officer Chew claimed to have fired at the machete-swinging teenager in self defense as he fell backwards into the bathtub, startled by Denovo's charge into the room. Some people believe him because he's a cop or because they knew Denovo. Others refuse to believe him for the same reasons.

If Chew's story is true, he may have been justified in pulling the trigger. But whether or not the shooting was indeed self-defense is less of an issue than why 26-year old Chew was there in the first place. In 1989, the Berkeley Police Review Commission upheld three complaints against Chew, then a Berkeley police officer – complaints that included charges of excessive force, abusive behavior, and improper arrests. In November, 1991, just nine months before he killed Denovo, Chew was shot several times by a fifteen-year-old robbery suspect.

The questions loom large. Why was Chew sent into the house? Why didn't the officer's police dog stop the five-foot-one, 105-pound Denovo as she allegedly burst into the bathroom? Why wasn't tear gas used to flush her out? Why didn't the UCPD make use of its trained negotiators?

A university statement issued on August 28 said that police weren't certain Denovo was still in the house; she might have fled while reinforcements were arriving. "Faced with the possibility that an armed, potentially dangerous person was prowling the campus, police decided to search the house," read the statement.

On September 24, an attorney for Denovo's Parents filed a complaint against the UC Police, charging that the UCPD failed to follow its own procedures for handling mentally disturbed suspects. The complaint said that the officers involved should have first attempted "mental health intervention or other intervention through her friends, parents, or attorney."

From the *East Bay Express*, December 18, 1992. *(Reprinted With Permission.)*

EDITORIALS

A quarter-century of mistakes

TWO LIVES, MORE THAN $2 million and far too much time, energy, and effort. People prosecuted for playing with chalk. Homeless people driven from one of the few safe havens they had. Ongoing clashes between police and protesters. Telegraph Avenue merchants wondering how long their windows will remain unshattered. That's the running tab so far in the battle over People's Park. By any standard it's way too high.

Clearly, the bulk of the blame lands at the feet of the university, which has arrogantly insisted on reclaiming the park just to prove it can, and the police forces that have inflicted the lion's share of the damage to humans. But some responsibility must also be taken by some protesters who have confused vandalism with politics and forgotten why People's Park was first founded.

Rosebud Abigail Denovo is the latest casualty in this tragedy. Her death was senseless. With the chancellor and his wife already safe, with five trained police officers, a stun gun, a dog, and the opportunity to negotiate instead of confront, there was no reason for shooting her four times. But the shots were not surprising: The police officer involved had already been cited by the city of Berkeley for using excessive force; he - like all California officers, according to Bud Stone, president of the Peace Officers Research Associates of California - had been trained to shoot to kill; and he had just returned to duty after surviving a shooting.

The decision to send the police in to find Denovo and bring her out practically determined the outcome.

We have yet to hear a convincing explanation from the university or the police why Denovo, alone in the house, could not have been drawn out using words, tear gas, or another non-lethal method. Why was Officer Craig Chew in the house with a loaded gun? Under the circumstances, we believe Denovo's death could have been avoided.

Of course, Denovo is not only a victim. Anyone who enters the home of the UC chancellor wielding a machete and charging an armed police officer, cannot be considered innocent. And the police have released evidence that this troubled woman fully expected - and perhaps welcomed - her fate. It would be wrong to make a hero or martyr of Denovo, as some activists have tried to do.

None of this exempts the university from the burden it must bear for creating and prolonging this horrible situation. Despite its claim that it wanted to work out a deal with the park activists, when push came to shove, the university was always shoving. Its argument for building on the park was that it had become crime-ridden. But if UC wanted to rid People's Park of crime, it could have done so without building volleyball and basketball courts, without inciting demonstrations and unleashing the police, without trampling on the First Amendment, without spending millions of dollars, and without killing two people. But UC has time and again demonstrated it would rather pay lawyers, cops, and overtime than put one cent into cleaning up the park.

Had it only poured the same resources and determination into realizing the dream of People's Park that it marshaled into destroying it, and the news of past week, much of the past year, and a good chunk of the past quarter-century would have been far different. It would have been better for all of us. Including Rosebud Abigail Denovo.

Officer in UC Shooting Was Subject of Probes

He was accused of misconduct 4 times

By Peter Fimrite and Mylene Mangalindan
Chronicle East Bay Bureau

The police officer who fatally shot an intruder inside the University of California at Berkeley chancellor's mansion had been investigated for using excessive force and for making improper arrests while serving on the Berkeley force, a police commissioner said yesterday.

Oakland police officer Craig Chew, 26, was accused of misconduct four times in 1989, when he was with the Berkeley Police Department. The Berkeley Police Review Commission upheld three of those complaints, said Robert Bailey, the commission's chief investigator. Bailey could not say whether disciplinary action was taken in any of the cases.

The misconduct charges came to light as police increased security on the campus and assigned an officer to shadow Chancellor Chang-Lin Tien and as more than 30,000 students returned to school. Rosebud Abigail Denovo, 19, an admitted revolutionary and People's Park supporter with a history of psychological problems and numerous run-ins with police, had made references in her diary to harming the Tiens. Police said the shooting was justified, but Denovo's friends defended her yesterday as a martyr who was murdered by police.

Master at Civil Disobedience

The woman's friends said that although she was a master at civil disobedience, she would not hurt anybody.

She may have wanted to "chop things up and smash the place," said Matt Little Moon, who was a friend. "But chopping up the chancellor and his wife into little, itty bitty pieces, that wasn't her style."

"People are enraged," said Maxina Ventura, a member of the People's Park Defense Committee. "Whether what she did was a good or bad thing to do is one issue, but we have to look at the actions of the police."

Denovo used a propane blowtorch to break through a basement window In the chancellor's home, setting off a silent alarm at 5:51 a.m. Tuesday, police said.

After a police officer spotted Denovo in the house, campus police called Tien and his wife, Di Hwa, and told them to lock their bedroom door. Berkeley police and canine units from the Oakland Police Department were then called in to help search the home.

After the chancellor and his wife were escorted from the building, canine units searched the second floor, where Denovo burst through a bedroom door and tried to slash Chew police said.

Chew reportedly fired three shots as he fell over a bathtub against the wall of an adjoining bathroom. Denovo was pronounced dead at 7:44 a.m.

Improper Arrests

Chew, who was a Berkeley policeman for three years before transferring to Oakland last year, was found to have made an improper arrest and used abusive behavior while breaking up an altercation between two couples on Telegraph Avenue on June 4,1989, Bailey said.

On July 16,1989, Chew used excessive force and made an improper arrest while breaking up a fight at the Bear's Lair pub on the Berkeley campus, Bailey said. Chew made another improper arrest while issuing a search warrant at a suspected drug house on Sept. 30, 1989, Bailey said.

David Beauvais, Denovo's attorney in several previous cases, said the misconduct charges make him wonder why Denovo, who was 5-foot-1 and weighed 105 pounds, was shot three times when a police dog should easily have been able to stop her.

Under standard operating rules, Chew has been placed on paid leave for three days. The investigation into the shooting is continuing, but police said Chew had no choice but to shoot.

"She tried to kill him, and he shot until the attack was stopped," said Oakland police Sergeant Brian Thiem.

Oakland chief backs policeman

Officer 'had no choice'

By Harry Harris
Tribune staff writer

An Oakland police officer's shooting of a machete wielding woman inside the home of the UC-Berkeley chancellor was "absolutely appropriate," Oakland Chief of Police George Hart said yesterday.

Hart said based on the evidence police have gathered, Officer Craig Chew "had no choice but to fire" the shots that killed Rosebud Abigail Denovo last Tuesday morning.

Denovo, 20, was shot three times when she attacked Chew in a bathroom at Chancellor Chang-Lin Tien's north campus home.

Police said Denovo, a self-described revolutionary, broke into the chancellor's home intending to kill him and his family. Security alarms detected her presence and Chew and his dog were requested by university police to help in a room-to-room search.

Hart said the fatal shooting "was tragic and I'm sure Officer Chew would be the first to express that sentiment. But the fact is the officer did what he had to do.

Hart also said media accounts of Chew's personnel record while a Berkeley police officer three years ago "are irrelevant to what happened."

It has been reported the Berkeley Police Review Commission upheld allegations of misconduct by Chew while he was a Berkeley officer in 1989.

They included making an improper arrest and abusing his discretion during a traffic stop in June 1989, and using excessive force and making an improper arrest while he was one of several officers breaking up a large brawl at the Bear's Lair pub on the university campus in July 1989.

The PRC also found Chew made an improper arrest during a raid on a drug house in September 1989.

see CHIEF, Back Page

Chief

Continued from page A-1

The July 1989 finding was upheld by the Berkeley city manager's office while the June finding was not. No decision has been made in the third case.

Hart said he has no reason to believe Chew is an overly aggressive officer.

The only time he fired his gun before this week's shooting was in July of last year when a 16-year-old robbery suspect shot him five times. Chew, who returned to full-time duty only a few months ago, was able to wound the assailant, who was later captured.

Hart said Chew's Berkeley record and his performance as an Oakland officer since he joined the department in November 1989 show him to be "a very capable and competent officer."

Hart said, "It's extremely unfortunate and inappropriate that some news stories have attempted to focus on allegations that Officer Chew had force-related complaints in his background" which "in my judgement are irrelevant to what happened at the chancellor's home.

"The fact is known by all and disputed by none that an emotionally disturbed person was attacking the officer and he had no choice but to do what he did. He was not at fault, and he should not be made a fall guy for that."

Hart said the media reports of Chew's past record is "misdirected focus that in my judgement gives comfort and support to those screwballs who are attempting to rationalize their rioting on the streets of Berkeley."

— Tribune staff writer Dan Vasquez contributed to this report.

Denovo 'would have killed me,' cop says

By Harry Harris and Paul Grabowics
Tribune staff writers

For Oakland police officer Craig Chew, the 20-year legacy of violent struggle over People's Park came down to a few seconds of life-and-death confrontation.

Chew remembers vividly the look on park protester Rosebud Denovo's face as she bore down on him with a machete in the cramped quarters of a bathroom in the home of University of California at Berkeley Chancellor Chang-Lin Tien.

Craig Chew says Rosebud Denovo
'had this really intense look.'

"I can only remember seeing her face. Her eyes were wide open and her mouth was open, like she was yelling something, but I can't remember what, if anything, she was saying," Chew told the Tribune last night in his first interview since he fatally shot Denovo on Tuesday.

"She just had this really intense look," he said.

Chew said he fired at Denovo as she burst into the bathroom, wildly swinging the machete and sending him reeling against a wall as he retreated.

"If I hadn't fallen backwards, she would have cut my arm or head off," the 26-year-old officer recalled. "The blade came only 6 inches from my upper torso.

"I didn't even have a chance to say anything" before he instinctively fired off four rounds, Chew said. "From the time she was in view until the time she fell was just a few seconds.

"I feel bad that it had to end up this way," Chew said. "Somebody forced me to take their life, but I refuse to die for somebody who's trying to kill me."

"It's not a good guy vs. bad guy thing, or police vs. somebody else. All the politics and all the reasons were gone. It's not for a cause. They are trying to take my life. They are trying to kill me."

Police say Denovo, who got into the chancellor's house by using a blowtorch to cut through a basement window, apparently planned to attack Tien and his wife.

A year ago Denovo had been charged with making bombs to blow up Tien's house and other targets because the university was building volleyball courts at People's Park.

The park has been the source of repeated clashes between protesters and police since May 1969, when the university evicted students and others from the site.

Chew was only 4 years old at the time.

But this week he found himself drawn into the controversy because of the Denovo shooting and his record as a police officer in Berkeley from 1988 to 1990.

Denovo's supporters have questioned why Chew had to shoot her, and pointed to past decisions by the Berkeley Police Review Commission upholding citizens' complaints against him for excessive force and improper arrests.

Chew dismissed those statements, saying, "In Berkeley, because of the

see OFFICER, Page A-9

From *The Oakland Tribune,* August 29, 1992. (Reprinted With Permission.)

OAKLAND TRIBUNE

Officer says he 'had no choice but to shoot'

Continued from Page A-1

political atmosphere, just being there... you're going to get complaints.... You get complaints whether they're justified or not."

Chew said in each case the police internal affairs section exonerated him and he was never disciplined by the city manager.

Oakland and Berkeley police have praised Chew's work as an officer and said his shooting of Denovo was justified.

Chew joined the Oakland force in November 1990, and last year was shot five times in a confrontation with a teenage robbery suspect.

He was called to the chancellor's mansion Tuesday morning because he is a canine-handler and UC-Berkeley police wanted a dog to search the house.

When Chew arrived, he said officers already had identified Denovo as the intruder and knew she was armed with a machete and knife.

"They were all just signs she was there to commit a murder and basically assassinate the chancellor and his wife," Chew said.

When he entered the house Chew said, the Tiens had locked themselves in their second-floor bedroom. With his gun drawn and his dog beside him, Chew said he joined other officers and searched the basement and ground floor of the mansion.

When they got to the second floor, some officers led the Tiens to safety, while Chew and other officers went inside another bedroom about 20 feet from where the Tiens had been.

The officers immediately sensed Denovo was nearby "because the dog was alerting on the door" to an adjacent bathroom, Chew said.

Chew said he went into the bathroom and was about to open a door to an adjoining bedroom and send the dog in, when Denovo "grabbed the handle" from the other side "and swung it open."

Chew said the dog then ran into the bedroom past Denovo.

'I feel bad that it had to end up this way. Somebody forced me to take their life, but I refuse to die for somebody who's trying to kill me.'

— **Craig Chew**
Oakland police officer

"It happened so fast that there was no opportunity to utilize the dog. He didn't have the opportunity to recognize the threat and engage (it)," Chew said.

Chew said Denovo then lunged at him with the machete before he could try to subdue her.

"It was physically impossible because I had my back against the wall and I was off balance," he said. "There's no way I can physically control her before she would have killed me.

"I had no choice but to shoot. No one wants to take someone's life, and no police officer wants to do it in their career," Chew said. "I don't want to do it again."

Despite having two close calls with death in the last year, Chew said he has no intention of leaving police work.

"I made a commitment to myself and the dog. It sounds kind of corny, but I don't want somebody else's actions to alter my goals."

Intruder at UC Home Was Shot in the Back

Attorney says autopsy raises serious questions

By Peter Fimrite
Chronicle Staff Writer

An autopsy report revealed yesterday that a machete-wielding intruder inside the chancellor's mansion at UC Berkeley was shot by a policeman four times, including once in the middle of the back.

The new details into the fatal August 25 shooting of 19-year-old activist Rosebud Abigail Denovo sparked another round of questions from lawyers and prompted police to defend the shooting.

Denovo, a 'self-styled revolutionary, used a blowtorch to break into the house of Chancellor Chang-Lin Tien and his wife, Di Hwa, early that morning. She had previously made references to harming the Tiens.

Alerted by a silent alarm, police evacuated the home and called in an Oakland canine unit to search the building. Officer Craig Chew, 26, shot Denovo after she burst through a second-floor bathroom door swinging a machete, police said.

Investigators originally reported that Chew fired four shots, but hit Denovo three

> *'The report reinforced our conclusion that the shooting was in self-defense'*
>
> — VICTORIA HARRISON
> UNIVERSITY POLICE CHIEF

times as he fell backwards into a bathtub.

The autopsy report shows, however, that Denovo. suffered four wounds: in the right side of the chest, right side of the neck, the back of the right shoulder and in the middle of her back. She also suffered "grazing" wounds to her left index finger and the "right fifth finger," the report stated. It does not specify the sequence of the shots or which of the wounds proved fatal.

The San Francisco Chronicle

Autopsy

from previous page

Results of a toxicology report, also released yesterday, show that Denovo was not under the influence of drugs or alcohol.

David Beauvais, a Berkeley lawyer who represented Denovo when she was arrested last year for possession of explosives, said the report raises serious questions about the police department's version of events.

"She was twice shot from behind or at least in the back area," said Beauvais, who plans to hire a pathologist to investigate. "This requires an explanation."

University police Chief Victoria Harrison said the results are consistent with the conclusions of investigators, statements by the officer who witnessed the shooting and the analysis of blood-splatter marks at the scene.

Harrison said Denovo's shoulder wound was the result of her swinging the machete across her body. She said the shot in the back probably occurred as she spun around and fell.

"The report reinforced our conclusion that the shooting was in self-defense," Harrison said. "The question 'Did he have to kill her?' is naive. He had two choices—be killed or defend himself."

Beauvais, meanwhile, has filed a written complaint against the university police for allegedly violating procedures in the Field Training Officer's Manual on handling "disturbed persons." He claims officers attempting to apprehend Denovo ignored provisions that they should stay calm, take plenty of time and use as little force as possible.

UC police Lieutenant Bill Foley said those rules did not apply because police did not know Denovo had any mental problems.

—Chronicle correspondent T. Christian Miller contributed to this report.

ROSEBUD

1973-1992

On the morning of Tuesday, August 25, Rosebud DeNovo was shot to death by police after entering the University of California Chancellor's mansion. This was after over a year of struggle between Rosebud, both personally and as part of the People's Park movement, and the UC police and administration.

Persecuted in her high school environment for her rejection of all authority and militant anarchist perspective, Rosebud left her home in Lexington, Kentucky, and traveled around the country. At the end of 1990 she settled in Berkeley, which she saw as a good starting point to become active in revolutionary politics. She resided in People's Park for a short time until she moved into a nearby house where many people lived rent-free. A few months later, Rosebud returned to life on the streets.

Rosebud took part in militant demonstrations during the war in Iraq, and was consistently active as people organized against the impending construction in People's Park in the spring of 1991. She was arrested several times during this period, for charges ranging from damaging a bank during anti-war protests, scamming on BART, and sleeping in People's Park. She was active in organizing an anti-July 4th rally in the Park as well as several other events, and participated nightly in the vigil on the People's Park sidewalk. On Telegraph Avenue she tabled for the Green Panthers, a small, loose network of militants for marijuana liberation. She developed a reputation as one of the most hardcore Southside agitators. This, combined with general police harassment of activists and homeless people (Rosebud was both), made her well known by police.

Shortly after the volleyball courts were constructed in the Park, involving several days of street fighting between Park defenders and multiple Bay Area police departments, Rosebud's life took a dramatic turn. While in custody for a minor protest offense, molotov cocktails and incriminating diaries found in a campsite in the Berkeley hills were linked to Rosebud by police, who charged Rosebud, her boyfriend Andrew Barnum, and Timothy Jacobs with heavy explosives charges. Jacobs was or became a police informer and made incriminating statements against Rosebud which the media used to smear her.

The University used the incident to create a large media spectacle hoping to embarrass the People's Park movement, creating front page stories in local dailies. Rosebud, 17 at the time the charges were filed, was transferred to a juvenile facility, where she was deprived of "adult" rights such as bail and visitors.

After two months, a study by the probation department determined that Rosebud should be tried as an adult, and Rosebud was returned to Santa Rita County Jail. Soon her bail was reduced to $10,000, after which her friends posted bond.

Once released, Rosebud moved to the Info Cafe, a radical live/work collective in North Oakland. Rosebud remained active in People's Park and the People's Park Annex, a vacant lot turned campground across from the Park. In her new role as public enemy #1, Rosebud was carefully watched by the police, and subjected to constant harassment. She was rearrested for resisting a police attack a month after her release but bailed out again quickly. Besides actively protesting the clearing of the

From *Slingshot*, Harvest Season Issue, 1992. (Reprinted With Permission.)

Annex, and the construction of the University designed Bathroom/guardhouse and the Basketball court in People's Park, Rosebud was active in the attempted construction of the People's Bathroom in the Park.

When Info Cafe disbanded in the spring of 1992, Rosebud and Andy moved to People's Park. Camping wherever at night, they spent their days in the grove just west of the driveway entrance. Increasing numbers of homeless people spent time at the grove, hanging out and talking about revolution-type stuff. Alarmed by the positive community in the grove, and the constant presence of Rosebud, University police kept a close watch on the grove, and dropped by to stare almost daily, arresting someone whenever possible.

Rosebud was especially hounded in the last days of her life, including an arrest in August. On Sunday night, August 23, Rosebud had to move after police came looking for her campsite, after they apparently overheard her describe its location earlier in the day. After the following night, early on Tuesday morning, Rosebud went to campus and broke into the Chancellor's mansion.

Little is known about what happened within the mansion. The Southside activist/ homeless community as well as Rosebud's family in Kentucky are demanding an independent investigation, but even if this takes place much will remain a mystery. We do know that Rosebud, from inside the mansion, called her friend Jim Henry, and said she thought her death was imminent and goodbye to everyone in the Park. We also apparently know that Rosebud was spotted by a UC cop through a window, who drew a gun and told her to drop her weapons. A machete and a knife were later found inside. The cop recognized Rosebud from previous arrests and believed that it was Rosebud who was inside. We have the police account, but the UC police have a continuous history of lies and distortions, as well as violence against activists.

According to police reports, Rosebud entered the mansion, armed with a machete and another knife, by cutting away a grating with a blowtorch, after dying her hair and donning medical gloves. She set off a silent alarm, after which police saw her through a window. Police called the Chancellor and told him to bolt his door, after which the cops moved in and evacuated the Chancellor. The UC police then brought in a K9 unit from the Oakland Police Department to find and capture Rosebud. Then, the police claim, as Rosebud was discovered she attacked the nearest cop, Craig Chew, with a machete knocking him into a bathtub. Chew then shot Rosebud in the hand, and fired three more shots, hitting Rosebud in the heart. An autopsy report is also pending.

Chew had just recently recovered from being shot five times by a burglar. He also had a history of complaints as a Berkeley cop including a sustained complaint by the Police Review Commission and the City Manager of excessive force stemming from a confrontation at the Bear's Lair, a campus pub. He may himself had a "itchy" trigger.

Of course, the police's version changes over time, and some details seem quite improbable, but we can't expect the police to publicly announce an extra-judicial execution. Rosebud was perhaps the People's Park activist they hated and feared the most, and she was trapped without a single possible witness. Calling officers from Oakland to finish the job suggests a fear of UC cops being held personally responsible by the community.

Normal police procedure would suggest encircling the house, followed by tear gas, calling her family or friends, calling a mediation team, even starving her out. Although UC police incompetence is common, the police had a motive and a willingness to kill Rosebud. An organizer of and inspiration to street people. A practitioner of direct action. An angry woman, not afraid to let them know. She had entered the Chancellor's mansion. This time, they decided not to arrest her.

LETTERS TO THE EDITOR

A Sad Ending

Editor—So sadly ends the tale of Rosebud A. Denovo. We have seen the rebels without a cause in the '50s, rebels with causes in the '60s and '70s, and rebels without purpose in the '80s and '90s.

When I first returned to the Bay Area 10 years ago, I made a pilgrimage to People's Park. The park that belonged to "the people" had become a mud hole inhabited by Reagan's schizophrenic homeless, drugged-out losers and their dealers, and burnt-out hippies who'd arrived in the same clothes 10 years before.

This was an insult to the memory of the freedom movement born in Berkeley. For people like Rosebud to be willing to die for what has become a rotting corpse of a long dead horse is a sad ending to a sad purposeless struggle.

Was this woman so deluded and grandiose to expect that her death would return the park to it's former "glory"? Sure people rioted and burned, but they have nothing better to do. Come on folks, join the world. People are dying for true freedom as millions of starving refugees shuffle in long lines from place to place because they're not in OPEC. AIDS is devastating the population of the Third World because the church wants unprotected sex and lots of babies. On and on and on.

And there is the brave warrior Rosebud, willing to kill or be killed in Berkeley for God's sakes over a dump cum volleyball court. What a sad statement. What a sad waste.

The rebels without purpose will riot at the drop of a hat in Berkeley. They've become caricatures of themselves. Maybe it's time to bury the dead horse and the poor deluded girl, and join the world, and let People's Park rest in peace.

From *The San Francisco Chronicle*, August 28, 1992. Letter by Michael S. Eckenrode.

Mental Health or Mental Abuse?
Rosebud DeNovo's Own Story

The following article was recently published by Humane Services for the Mentally-crisised, a social/political organization for the better care of the mentally crisised, an organization that Rosebud had a growing interest in. Rosebud wrote it for the Humane Services for the Mentally-crisised newsletter shortly prior to her death. Certainly, Rosebud would want the public to be aware of the abuses people experience in psychiatric facilities.

I was committed to Charter Ridge Hospital at the age of 14 by my parents, about four years ago. I spent nine months there. I was not in there because of any real illness; I was there because (basically) I did not get along with my parents and other authority figures. Because of my age, I could not fight this commitment legally.

I was on a unit which housed about 12 young teenagers at any given time. Everyone was between 11 and 15, and the average length of stay was three months. Out of everyone who was on the unit with me while I was there, only one person was diagnosed with an adult mental illness.

The rules were very strict. We had strict limits on what kind of personal property was allowed and who we could communicate with. No physical contact was allowed, not even a hug. There was a long list of subjects we were not allowed to discuss.

Isolation, which was supposed to be used only when a person was an immediate danger to self or others, was used regularly as a punishment for refusing to follow staff's orders. I was placed in isolation several times. Restraints and drugs were used similarly, although I was never drugged myself.

Almost everyone on the unit was required to take some kind of medication. I was able to refuse to take anything, but I was an exception.

People who were new to the unit or who had attempted to run, or who were considered suicidal, were monitored constantly by staff. I was required, when I first arrived, to sleep in the hallway and was observed even when taking a shower.

Eventually, I managed to get out by going along with the program and convincing staff I would no longer make trouble. Two years later I had two other experiences with mental hospitals, which were worse.

Both of these places were similar to Charter Ridge. Misuse of isolation and restraint was even more common. I knew several people who were physically assaulted by staff. One friend of mine who attempted to run away was strapped down for three days without food or water.

Many people who were committed to these institutions became almost like zombies, with their entire personalities changed. Others became suicidal. Those who emerged relatively psychologically normal were usually able to withstand the mental abuse by uniting with other teenagers there. Fortunately, I was strong enough to remain myself, but these experiences had a lasting, damaging effect on me.

"...shot, Harvest Season Issue, 1992. (Reprinted With Permission.)

UNIVERSITY OF CALIFORNIA
POLICE DEPARTMENT
BERKELEY

FIELD TRAINING MANUAL

C. Handling Disturbed Persons   TRAINEE

Never rush blindly into the situation. Take time
out to look over the situation, ask questions,
find out all you can about the sick person. Call
for assistance. Use the City of Berkeley's mental health workers, if appropriate. Delay of
time will often serve a double purpose. If the
mentally disturbed person is excited, the pas-
sage of time will permit the person to calm
down. While waiting for the arrival of addition-
al assistance, formulate a plan of action. How
will the person be removed? Who shall enter the
room? Are the escape routes from the house properly covered? Keep cool, calm, and wait.

1. Use as little force as possible.
2. Ignore verbal abuse.
3. Avoid excitement.
4. Do not deceive.
5. Restrain and calm down.

LONG LIVE ROSEBUD

PEOPLES PARK ACTIVIST EXECUTED BY BERKELEY, OAKLAND, UNIVERSITY OF CALIFORNIA POLICE ON AUGUST 25, 1992 AT THE BEHEST OF CHANCELLOR CHANG-LIN TIEN IN HIS RESIDENCE FOR UNLAWFUL ENTRY; AGE 19, WEIGHT 97LBS., FEMALE, ANARCHIST

HONOR ROSEBUD

FRIDAY, AUGUST 25TH IS THE THIRD ANNIVERSARY OF ROSEBUD DENOVO'S DEATH FROM POLICE BULLETS WHILE FIGHTING FOR PEOPLE'S PARK AND HERSELF. JOIN US TO REMEMBER HER AND HER VISION FOR ANARCHY IN PEOPLE'S PARK.

Friday 7:00 People's Park

Stop the war!!

Against:
* Homeless People
* Radical Youth
* Angry Women
* Teenage Immigrant Welfare Mothers on Drugs

Sponsored by
Wingnut

International

Normal person, we will get you!

SLINGSHOT

IMPORTANT
ELECTION
COVERAGE
Page17

Issue Number 47   **Berkeley, California**   **Harvest Season 1992**

ROSEBUD
1973-1992

On the morning of Tuesday, August 25, Rosebud DeNovo was shot to death by police after entering the University of California Chancellor's mansion. This was after over a year of struggle between Rosebud, both personally and as part of the People's Park movement, and the UC police and administration.

Persecuted in her high school environment for her rejection of all authority and militant anarchist perspective, Rosebud left her home in Lexington, Kentucky, and travelled around the country. At the end of 1990 she settled in Berkeley, which she saw as a good starting point to become active in revolutionary politics. She resided in People's Park for a short time until she moved into a nearby house where many people lived rent-free. A few months later Rosebud returned to life on the streets.

Rosebud took part in militant demonstrations during the war in Iraq, and was consistently active as people organized against the impending construction in People's Park. During this period, for charges ranging from damaging a bank during anti-war protests, scamming on BART, and sleeping in People's Park. She was active in organizing an anti-July 4th rally in the Park as well as several other events, and participated nightly in the vigil on the People's Park sidewalk. On Telegraph Avenue she tabled for the Green Panthers, a small, loose network of militants

for marijuana liberation. She developed a reputation as one of the most hardcore Southside agitators. This, combined with general police harassment of activists and homeless people (Rosebud was both), made her well known by police.

Shortly after the volleyball courts were constructed in the Park, involving several days of street fighting between Park defenders and multiple Bay Area police departments,

was or became a police informer and made incriminating statements against Rosebud which the media used to smear her.

The University used the incident to create a large media spectacle hoping to embarrass the People's Park movement, creating front-page stories in local dailies. Rosebud, 17 at the time the charges were filed, was transferred to a juvenile facility, where she was deprived of "adult" rights such as bail and visitors.

Rage erupts at UC Berkeley following Rosebud's death

Rosebud's life took a dramatic turn. While in custody for a minor protest offense, molotov cocktails and incriminating diaries found in a campsite in the Berkeley hills were linked to Rosebud by police, who charged Rosebud, her boyfriend Andrew Barnum, and Timothy Jacobs with heavy explosives charges. Jacobs

After two months, a study by the probation department determined that Rosebud should be tried as an adult, and Rosebud was returned to Santa Rita County Jail. Soon her bail was reduced to $10,000, after which her friends posted bond.

Once released, Rosebud moved to the Info Cafe, a radical live/work collective in North Oakland. Rosebud remained active in People's Park and the People's Park Annex, a vacant lot turned campground across from the Park. In her new role as public enemy #1, Rosebud was carefully watched by the police, and subjected to constant harassment. She was rearrested for resisting a police attack a month after her release but bailed out again quickly. Besides actively protesting the clearing of the Annex, and the construction of the University

continued on page 9

1992

PROTEST 500 YEARS OF GENOCIDE

OCTOBER 11, 1992 SAN FRANCISCO, CA

AQUATIC PARK, FISHERMAN'S WHARF

DEMONSTRATION

CIVIL DISOBEDIENCE

Rosebud's Mission

Denial; shock, horror... then questions... Why did she go in there? What was to be gained? How does it all fit together?

Chaos Calling

I have known Rosebud closely for over a year. I felt an unearthly kinship with her; like Rosebud I had a teenage experience in a white, upper middle class suburban environment dominated by conflict with parents, teachers, and the mental health system, and I faced almost total alienation from my high school classmates. At the age of fifteen I was possessed by a revolutionary vision; I felt called by mysterious spirits of the wild to wage war upon "the system," upon America, upon all that suppressed the fire of the spirit and the magic of the forest. I became facinated by Anarchist philosophy revolutionary struggles around the world

Unlike Rosebud I did not run away; I chose to bide my time, and perhaps that is why I'm still alive. About a decade has passed and although I have tried to live by this primal vision I have faltered along the way and my inspiration has become a memory. I strain desperately to bring to mind. The more I realised that Rosebud was currently in tune with the same energies I once was, the more I strove to understand her vision, her philosophy, her understanding of an all-encompassing plan that was once so clear to me.

Although Rosebud died in accordance with her values, the inhability of her vision was suddenly cut short. Rosebud was continually reading, studying, and

developing her ideas; given more years her perspective may have evolved to significantly greater clarity. Given the sensational ignorance of the media and general popular confusion as to the meanings of her life, I want as many people as possible to understand what she was about, to think about her intense but often irresfutable message. Regardless of what conflicts you may have with her beliefs, her experience may help to transform your worldview.

Rosebud on Revolution

Rosebud's life, her philosophy, her analysis of the world and her surroundings was almost completely focused on the idea of a social-political revolution that would profoundly change every aspect of our existance; the society we experience now was considered worthless in terms of significant, meaningful fostering of freedom and dignity. All that was worthwhile in the end was the bringing about of the great transformation.

Rosebud could not easily communicate the world she wanted to create; our language in not sufficient to explain it, and she would easily admit her own perspective was still a bit removed from a post-revolutionary perspective. Many who talked with her could not see her vision behind her teenage hard-core attitude. She did know she wanted a thoroughly cooperative, non-hierarchical society, in which all people could freely seek to fulfill their full potential.

A lot of people talk carelessly about revolution, armed struggle, and radical change. Rosebud was one of very, very few people who

would stare in the face global class war, the massive, universal suffering inplicit in a total, rapid rearrangement of the world, and the explosion of the anger of everyone who was ever dragged down hard by those in privilege; and simply say "yes."

This is about destruction on a collosal scale, as an unavoidable price of a tolerable world, about people from all walks of life calling down an apocalypse on those complicit in the dynamics of power.

The Individual as Weapon

Rosebud wanted to bring this all about through the effort of individuals and small autonomous groups of outlaws. Freed from the restraints imposed by social conditioning and fear, one person has the potential to unleash great chaos and disruption upon the system. Individual acts can smash weak points in the fabric holding the repressive society together.

As an example, the life of Rosebud was clearly focused on and disciplined toward the achievement of revolutionary objectives. She was not a drinker, unlike most self-proclaimed revolutionaries, and despite her involvement in the marijuana liberation movement, she was not a heavy stoner. She was not tempted by any of the lures of materialist America.

Yet she believed in guerilla warfare as a calling for ordinary people. People from a wide cross-section of backgrounds were inspired by her to greater resistance. It is significant that in all her alleged guerilla activity, the only weapons cited were gasoline,

a machete, and her bare hands. Although sure she did her best to survive the mor August 25, despite the conjecturing of she was ready to make the ultimate sac After all, many would perish in the cata she called for (maybe everyone if it happen), so her own life was a fair pri what she asked for.

What holds us all back is our fe sense of hopelessness. Rosebud s potential chain reaction of drastic, desp individual attacks. Perhaps she could cause a few random events in a se mediocrity, or maybe be in hundreth moni armed chaos.

Non-Conclusion

When the man shot Rosebud do opened a Pandora's Box he hasn't a char understanding. The uprising in her wake limited only by initial numbers and unpreparedness of people for such a d event. As the week after her death came a those demonstrating in her support: exba from those in her own Berkeley South community to include many disaffe teenagers who identify with her spir absolute resistance and the repression experienced at the hands of the autho And it ain't over yet.

And that's only the short term have yet to see what takes place when p really think about Rosebud's life and "What just happened?" As many old rac have noted, once resistance is fully presen

continued on page

Mental Health or Mental Abuse?
Rosebud DeNovo's Own Story

The following article was recently published by Humane Services for the Mentally-ceased, a social/political organization for the better care of the mentally-criseased, an organization that Rosebud had a growing interest in Rosebud wrote it for the Humane Services for the Mentally-ceased newsletter shortly prior to her death. Certainly, Rosebud would want the public to be aware of the abuses people experience in psychiatric facilities.

I was committed to Charter Ridge Hospital at the age of 14 by my parents, about four years ago. I spent nine months there. I was not in there because of any real illness; I was there because (basically) I did not get along with my parents and other authority figures. Because of my age, I could not fight this commitment legally.

I was on a unit which housed about 12 young teenagers at any given time. Everyone was between 11 and 15, and the average length of stay was three months. Out of everyone who was on the unit with me while I was there, only one person was diagnosed with an adult mental illness.

The rules were very strict. We had strict limits on what kind of personal property was allowed and who we could communicate with. No physical contact was allowed, not even a hug. There was a long list of subjects we were not allowed to discuss.

Isolation, which was supposed to remain only when a person was an immediate danger to self or others, was used regularly as a punish-

ment for refusing to follow staff's orders. I was placed in isolation several times. Restraints and drugs were used similarly, although I was never drugged myself.

Almost everyone on the unit was required to take some kind of medication. I was able to refuse to take anything, but I was an exception

People who were new to the unit or who had attempted to run, or who were considered suicidal, were monitored constantly by staff. I was required, when I first arrived, to sleep in the hallway and was observed even when taking a shower.

Eventually, I managed to get out by going along with the program and convincing staff I would no longer make trouble. Two years later I had two other experiences with mental hospitals, which were worse.

Both of these places were similar to Charter Ridge. Misuse of isolation and restraint was even more common. I knew several people who were physically assaulted by staff. One friend of mine who attempted to run away was strapped down for three days without food or water.

Many people who were committed to these institutions became almost like zombies, with their entire personalities changed. Others became suicidal. Those who emerged relatively psychologically normal were usually able to withstand the mental abuse by uniting with other teenagers there. Fortunately, I was strong enough to remain myself, but these experiences had a lasting, damaging effect on me.

In the spirit of
Demonstrators show anger in street action after the kil

The evening of Rosebud DeNovo's death about 150 people gathered in People's Park. Many rumors had been in the air all day about the killing of Rosebud with many different perspectives on the tragedy. but there was a general consensus that the police didn't have to kill Rosebud. Many emotions were flowing from shock to sadness to rage.

A few UC Bureaucrats, including UC PR person Milton Fuji, showed up and sparked an angry reaction from people gathered. Many people got in their faces and told them to "get the fuck outta here" and as Fuji was leaving he got hit in the back with a cardboard garbage can. Fuji, being a good UC stooge, later wrote an incredibly propagandistic column printed in

the Oakland Tribune and the Daily Cal, 1 People's Park activists were a racist lyn mob. Many people responded with letters i columns to Fuji's utter bullshit.

A little while later a short march to the police station of about 200 people happer with people chanting and shouting in grief a rage. The scene was tense but eventua people filtered away to later regather at park.

People gathered in the Park at 9 p.m. w lots of cops and media lurking around. Ma homeless people and street youth, we generally don't come to protests, showed up full force and were visibly upset abo Rosebud's murder. Many people urg

Sunday: Mud people dance and grunt on Telegraph

WHY?

People have questioned why a homeless woman who hung around People's Park would creep into the UC chancellor's mansion with a machete and a note that said all construction out of the park. What's the connection and why now?

Invading somebody's home is not new for the US; it's how this country was begun and how it's power has been spread around the world. The economy has been grown and maintained with invasions into other people's realities. Is invasion only ok for rich men in positions of power?. The obliteration of the homes that use to exist on the land of People's Park was the university's attempt to displace anarchists of the late 60's. The nightly displacement of the homeless in People's Park by UCity police now is another example.

UC regents, who sit on boards of various war-making corporations, claimed the land by

'eminent domain' and have employed state police as an occupying army. The growth of the corporate military state has produced the growing number of poor and homeless. The collaboration between the city and the university police and administration in the development of the UC Long Range Development Plan is designed to protect the bio-chemical warfare experimentation that is now replacing nuclear warfare.

The university is beginning another year training another generation of authoritarians and two dimensional corporate robots and their support system of "professionals". At a time of info-tainment when little of media reflects what is real, and anyone can see that what is being done so far is not going to make any real change in the direction of and momentum of this death machine that hates people and believes in professionalism, Rosebud wanted something real to happen to cause real change. Maybe Rosebud just couldn't lie to herself the way most people do and say compromise with this system won't hurt for another generation.   Nancy Delaney

ROSEBUD 1973-1992

gned Bathroom/guardhouse and the etball court in People's Park, Rosebud active in the attempted construction of 'eople's Bathroom in the Park.

When Into Cafe disbanded in the spring of , Rosebud and Andy moved to People's Camping wherever at night, they spent days in the grove just west of the wsy entrance. Increasing numbers of eless people spent time at the grove, ing out and talking about revolution-type Alarmed by the positive community in grove, and the constant presence of bud, University police kept a close watch e grove, and dropped by to stare almost e arresting someone whenever possible. osebud was especially hounded in the last of her life, including an arrest in August. iunday night, August 23, Rosebud had to e after police came looking for her site, after they apparently overheard her ribe its location earlier in the day. After lowing right early on Tuesday morning, bud went to campus and broke into the cellor's mansion.

tle is known about what happened within nansion. The Southside activist/homeless unity as well as Rosebud's family in

Kentucky are demanding an independent investigation, but even if this takes place much will remain a mystery.

After the Fall

The breath is silent

Now,

But hear the beat

Of that disembodied heart

As stout and

Sure and

Clear as a

Blazing Nova

No wonder

Evil trembles

Still.

eli yates

Rosebud, from inside the mansion, called her friend Jim Henry, and said she thought her death was imminent and good-bye to everyone in the Park. We also apparently know that Rosebud was spotted by a UC cop through a window, who drew a gun and told her to drop her weapons. A machete and a knife were later found inside. The cop recognized Rosebud from previous arrests and believed that it was Rosebud who was inside. We have the police account, but the UC police have a continuous history of lies and distortions, as well as violence against activists.

According to police reports, Rosebud entered the mansion, armed with a machete and another knife, by cutting away a grating with a blowtorch, after dying her hair, and donning medical gloves. She set off a silent alarm, after which police saw her through a window. Police called the Chancellor and told him to bolt his door, after which the cops moved in and evacuated the Chancellor. The UC police then brought in a K9 unit from the Oakland Police Department to hunt and capture Rosebud. Then, the police claim, as Rosebud was discovered she attacked the nearest cop,

continued from page 1

continued on back page

ebud
d have wanted it that way

nge, while others argued against it. g the angry discussion an individual ed to saw on the volleyball courts. pling many others to start doing damage e courts. The police moved in, clubbing d people and the response for many was hand to hand with the cops.

a tense atmosphere had erupted. Cops ked one person unconscious and sters responded with some rock ing. Several arrests were made ding John Vance and Andy Barnum bud's boyfriend). Barnum is still in jail.

few minutes later a bonfire broke out on corner of Telegraph and Haste and a of about 100 people gathered. At this the cops laid back. Down Haste people ng ripping down construction wood from ew UC dorm at 2424 Channing and a barricade was built and set on fire. Many le began throwing rocks at the police. le joined in and the crowd was ly defiant and noticeably diverse ting homeless, youth, activists, people of students and women.

s police formed skirmish lines they moved d the crowd attempting to disperse it. crowd broke down into smaller, mobile ps. Protesters moved around the side running from police charges, setting es in several intersections, making ades, attempting to overturn a police and smashing at least two others. At ent points in the night people openly

chased police away making for a angry celebration.

At one point in the night people began inflicting damage on a UC construction site on Durant near Shattuck. Police finally scattered the rioters using vehicles and officers on foot in tandem. A number of arrests occured throughout the night.

People's anger was extremely focused against the police and the UC. No looting occurred despite the generic claims of the media who potrayed the night as just "Another Riot in Berkeley". The riot was both unified and militant and did have a real sense of purpose even if the purpose was to do some

Sunday crowd faces police skirmish line–spot the donut

damage. People felt powerful.

Though there was sense of wanting to avenge Rosebud's killing and many people felt Rosebud would have wanted us to riot, the rebellion went deeper than a police killing or People's Park or hatred of the police and UC. It was about daily anger and frustration and trying to reclaim some spirit against the alienation, misery, and repression of this rotten system that denies human potential and its ability to create something better

More Demonstrations

Another gathering occured the next evening, Wednesday. After spending some

continued on page 16

What Would Emma Say About Rosebud?

Over 90 years ago, Leon Czolgosz, an anarchist, assassinated President McKinley. He was widely condemned, both in the mainstream press and in most of the left, as at best insane, if not a total monster. Almost alone, Emma Goldman rose to his defense, speaking and organizing on his behalf. There are, of course, many differences between his case and that of Rosebud, not least that he succeeded whereas there is only police conjecture that Rosebud even planned an attempt; Czolgosz got a "fair trail" complete with defense attorneys who apologized for their unpleasant duty before being electrocuted by the state while Rosebud was summarily executed on the spot. Nonetheless, what Emma wrote concerning that case seems strikingly appropriate to repeat.

"Leon Czolgosz and other men of this type, far from being depraved creatures of low instinct are in reality supersensitive beings unable to bear up under too great social stress. They are driven to some violent expression, even at the sacrifice of their own lives, because they cannot supinely witness the misery and suffering of their fellows. The blame for such acts must be laid at the door of those who are responsible for the injustice and inhumanity which dominate the world. ...My heart goes out to him in deep sympathy, as it goes out to all the victims of oppression and misery, to the martyrs past and future that die, the forerunners of a better and nobler life."

Chapter One

Rosebud Remembers

on't cry Andy, don't cry.
Wait Andy, my heart fell into the ocean.
They're going to lock me up.
Don't let them lock me up, Andy.
They said only two years.
I wouldn't live for two years.
It would turn my soul into an empty soup kitchen."

"Hush little sweetie, it'll be all right. Let's go to sleep."

"Andy, I need space tonight. I need to be alone to think."

So he left her in her sleeping bag in the Berkeley Hills and the cops chased her out only an hour later. Only an hour later. What if. Arrival of the What Ifs.

See, when anyone dies, everybody who is left begins to go over the "What if I had done this and what if I had done that?" So what did the death of Rosebud mean and where is she if she didn't believe in heaven? What killed her and who killed her? If it turns out that we all did, how could it have been different?

They are lowering small warriors into the ground. The seasons change every day some years. They are turning freedom into jail terms and all the white rabbits have gone into hiding. Andy said she was scared before she died. He had seen her that night. Only a few hours later she was to break into the UC Chancellor's mansion, determined to be Joan of Arc and Emma Goldman all in one. She and Andy had an on again off again relationship and that night it was on. They were being good to each other, they were being friends. They didn't sleep together that night, Rosebud said she needed a bit of space. Sometimes she needed to be alone for a while, so Andy left. She was terrified because the jail thing was hanging over her. They were threatening her with two years and he said that would have killed her in a different way. She couldn't have stood not being free.

So he said good-bye and she said not a word about what was going to happen later. Maybe she didn't know what she was going to do, maybe it was a last minute desperate thought based on not having gotten any rest at all that night. Because after Andy left, the cops came. They'd found out where she was sleeping in the hills so they came to tell her to get moving. They didn't offer to help her get to a place where she could keep her stuff, they just plain said "leave". If you didn't have a home there was no place left in Berkeley where it was legal to sleep, so if they wanted they could bust you. And they were always after Rosebud because she was a known activist. Even though she was only four foot eleven and ninety seven pounds, they considered her a danger.

> I pledge revulsion to the scab
> on the United Fates of America
> and to the asshole on which it lands
> one vacation, under Sod
> with racism and injustice
> before the Fall.

Tis a gift to be an anarchist
tis a gift to be free
tis a gift to come down
to where you ought to be.
Don't cry, Andy. Don't cry.
Don't cry Mom and Daddy.
Rosebud's with God now.

But Rosebud hadn't believed in God. She was a tiny smiling anarchist with a sense of humor and an Emma Goldman goal. Don't start in about God. Andy, I couldn't tell you what I was going to do because I didn't know what I was going to do. When you left I thought it would be okay, my public defender would get me off and you'd have your check. We'd go someplace where they wouldn't chase us at night. It would be warm and the trees would smell nice. The cops would be far away in Copsville and we'd have smokes and a Walkman with fresh batteries and stuff to read. I said I just needed some space. I didn't know the cops would yank me out at four AM and say "get moving". How could I get moving? I had all my stuff, I had to leave most of it.

Rosebud Abigail Denovo was nineteen years old when she was shot to death. Where were the negotiators, the bull horns, the usual attempts to bring out a suspect known to be in a house that was empty?

Chapter Two
Elisa Remembers

'm Rosebud's friend. We were both anarchists. We'd go on demonstrations. During one demonstration I went to, there were more than a hundred rounds that went into the crowd and one person was shot so close to the jugular vein that it's very lucky he didn't die. Ten more people were shot in the stomach and other vital organs. We walked around to where this happened. Five people were brought into a corner bar, and they were on top of a pool table. They were bleeding, and the blood was all over the pool table and all over the floor.

The friends of the injured people called the hospital for an ambulance but the ambulance people said, "No, we're not gonna come until the police tell us to." So they called back three different times and nobody came. And so at that point they just took the doors off the hinges and brought the people to the hospital. They just ran with the people on top of these doors and random boards to get them to the hospital. That demonstration was to protest some injustices. Rosebud wasn't with me then.

We were trying to do squats, we'd break into abandoned houses so homeless people could have a place to stay. We also ran a cafe and an info shop in Berkeley called the Long Haul, we'd carry alternative press books like a library.

Did you meet Rosebud at an action? Did you ever live with her? How did you become friends?

OK. She came around to the People's Park in the Spring of '91 and she started to be one of those familiar faces. You know there's like always the same people at the demonstrations and the same people in the park. So she became one of those, and we just became friends. Like, because of that we'd be at an event and we'd be saying, "Oh, no one else came. Only the regular wing nuts are here. And so we'd pretty much be like diehards, you know, we'd show up even if we knew it was gonna be a pathetic event. It's strange, Rosebud was always there.

Rosebud was dedicated...?

Yeah, she was everywhere. People would say, "Oh, I have to give this to Rosebud. She's gonna be at this rally on that demonstration tonight, so they'd give it to her then." You know, that sort of thing.

What was the happiest moment or the happiest day that you ever spent with her?

Well, we had worked together on the anti-Fourth of July smoke-in a couple of years ago. Only she was in jail when it actually happened. So it was kind of sad because, you know, she was looking forward to it, and she'd put a lot of work into it. She'd written and posted the flyers. So she got out of jail and we picked her up, and we were laying on my bed just looking at the ceiling. We were both really tired and half asleep.

Oh gosh, OK. I'll try to get myself together here. We were saying how we felt that we were dissolving, while we were looking at the ceiling, you know. And we were feeling ourselves like really heavy and really light at the same time, and saying, "Oh, you know, we're dissolving." And like saying how much we really needed each other.

And it wasn't just us like two separate people—it was more like, you know, we were the movement. We were part of a group of people with familiar faces who stick up for each other and are struggling together, but are also having fun together. It's like a really great thing, you know, to be acknowledged by your group. But it was really scary too because, well, she'd just gotten out of jail. So there was her depression around that.

She used to call us from jail, and always really early in the morning because she knew we'd be there. And she'd want to know how things were, what was going on and what people were doing, and what was going on in People's Park. You know, "How's the Park?" and that sort of thing.

She would always say, "It's just so good to know that you're there, and to know there's someone you can count on." She knew that she could call us. She saw that most people in jail are isolated and spoke about that a lot. She was meaning it was OK that there was a support group of people like us that she was a part of. And she could rely on that. It was like a feeling of hope and survival and that sort of thing, you know.

So I guess I remember being in my room, you know, having this weird moment. But it was really nice! It was scary, but also really nice. It was scary because, you know, it was kind of like touching the lowest points we might have felt in our life, but also like kind of feeling at the root of what we're like trying to do. It makes me so upset and so sad when I'm thinking about it. Oh!

You can cry. It's OK. I guess the day that you heard what had happened, you must have been pretty shocked.

I was sleeping, and a friend came in to tell us. It was so early. It's almost kind of funny because that's always how she called, you know. If she called from jail we'd be in bed, you know. We'd answer the phone and it would be her. And Peter would be next to me asleep and it was the same way it was when we found out that she died. And he was saying "Rosebud's dead. Rosebud's dead." It didn't...I thought I was dreaming. It didn't make sense at all.

You know, she used to always tell us about things she wanted to do. She used to talk a lot of stuff, you know. She was really militant, and I don't know if she was joking. She used to say things like "Oh, this needs to be destroyed over here." And she had really strong language, you know.

OK. So I heard that she was dead. You know, Peter said it, and he had to say it several times since I was looking away so it didn't register at first. And it didn't sound real. I couldn't take it, you know. I couldn't. It couldn't be true because, well, it just couldn't. And I was picturing like, you know, her size and like, you know, me being also small, a little woman too. Her kind of gentleness. It was just sort of crazy, how could it be? I was just thinking of her heart, you know, and I was like picturing how strong and how fragile it was at the same time. It's so weird that she was shot in the heart. And like picturing that, you know, was just so strange. It's kind of hard, kind of unclear right now.

I think Nick had found out on the radio that it happened. It just didn't seem real for a long time and even later it didn't even seem real. I wasn't even crying. I was more in shock than anything. I was just like…wrong. I couldn't accept it.

Everyone was going then to the Memorial Demonstration. I wanted to hear it at the park and find out if it was real, you know. I just had to get to the park right away. And then I saw Eli, and we just, you know, hugged each other, and then we went to the place where she used to hang out a lot. And everyone was there. That's when it first started to seem real.

We saw Steve and her boyfriend, Andy. You know, I always was her best friend, at least out here. Some people had said that Rosebud was a wing nut. She wasn't. She was just too bright for her own good. Andy was in bad shape. He was all broken up.

At the memorial a cop insulted her memory and Andy couldn't contain himself. He hit the cop so he landed in jail from August to Christmas.

You know, there's always a few people that are going to take action about what they think is wrong. So the law is always gonna be following them around. See Rosebud was one of them.

What happened was like the whole way her life had been up to that point. You know, her survival depended on the Movement, and it was so urgent that it would take these forms. Like things to fight for her causes. She always had to be on the offensive because, you know, she was always being attacked by the cops.

There's a lot of pain. Everybody I've spoken to has said that even though the newspapers described her as emotionally disturbed, that she was so together. Nobody describes her as a wing nut. She never seemed like that to anybody in all the people that knew her here.

Yes. When I think of Rosebud, I think of, well—you know, she was so driven! All day she'd be walking around doing or planning actions. You know, she had a notebook, and had her list of all the things she was gonna do that day. Most of the times I remember running into her she'd be saying, "I'm going to make this flyer or that poster. I'm gonna go table for this, and mail out those notices." And that's what she was always doing, you know. Her day was always doing things for the movement.

It wasn't like "I have to go to work," or, you know, " I have this love relationship and thus and so is happening in it." She didn't have so much of a personal ego like, you know most people. She didn't think that this stuff mattered much. Her idea of herself and what she needed was so intermingled with revolutionary change. The most important things in her life were revolutionary actions, you know.

Being free and being wild, and being alive was like, the thing you know, that she needed to be. And so, since it wasn't that way, (she was facing jail again) it was gonna be like doing whatever needed to be done to make it that way. Most people wouldn't put themselves in that kind of danger or dedicate all the time to these projects, like Rosebud.

So you want to know how she was—she'd say things like, "Oh, I need a jacket." Like she would just mention it in the circle of all us friends that were, you know, in her struggle. Then she'd wait and it would come to her. Maybe it wouldn't be a specially pretty jacket. But she didn't really care about being pretty anyway, you know. She had this intense sense of purpose. She wasn't a drifter.

Chapter Three

Everyone Remembers I

his act became the event that would inflame People's Park activists forever. It was the most Rosebud could do.

Oh Rosebud, were you Orson Welles' sled in Citizen Kane or the actual flower itself for which the sled was named? Memory being the long ice crusher of thought, the complex bubble of past events that break into the new moments of our lives.

I, Rosebud, who believed in no heaven or hell, nothing but the one encountered here, want to tell you, Mama, Daddy and Andy, that I'm in heaven. Emma Goldman's here, making gingersnaps for poor Leon Czolgoz who shot President McKinley, and there's some really rich people waiting on us hand and foot, just like Yukon Hannibal in the Park said they would.

Tell my friends in the park that although they thought they shot me, I'm still there.

Go past the grove into the open space and then at the side closest to Amoeba Records, there'll be some plum trees. Down past where Jim Henry and my other friends planted this memorial garden for me where the red petunias made it but the blue and white ones wilted.

Check out the Free Box. Every time UC tore it down, I'd start to build it again.

Okay, what's the big deal about People's Park of Berkeley?

It's only the origin of the Free Speech Movement in America. In 1969 thousands of people marched down Telegraph Avenue chanting "We want the Park". In 1991 when the cops, on UC orders, started taking down the Free Boxes, the word went out again.

Remember when you were five my child, and told us how politically incorrect we were. When you were nine my daughter, and decided to step so far inside your mind to that place where we called to you but you never answered.

When you were reaching for the liberty of puberty and we panicked and obeyed the shrink. We didn't know the psych unit would drive you crazy. We didn't know the stuff you saw would make you quoth the raven nevermore.

They told us they could help our family so unto them we gave our only begotten daughter…

—hoping to undo the trouble…

—hoping to tame Rosebud Abigail Denovo. You had named yourself so that the initials spelled RAD.

Sweet smiling jaunty little figure, missed forever like a dark stain of pain on a firefly's wing. Broken wing.

Sing for this sad craving in my gut of worrying, wondering, what went wrong what did I do? Backtracking, pondering, was there something, anything, what could have averted it? What kind of happy life could you have had?

Rosebud left her home in Lexington Kentucky when she was a young teenager and journeyed around the country. She stayed in Berkeley first at the end of 1990. She was a wanted child, her father taught at a small college. They didn't understand her being so different.

We didn't understand your rebellions. We listened to the voice of authority. We worried when we visited you because yes it did seem like a jail, that hospital unit. We thought you were sick and doctors could help you. Like you had appendicitis or something. The doctors said you needed help.

Rosebud settled in Berkeley because she had read a lot and what she had read made her decide to become an anarchist. There were lots of anarchists in Berkeley and many of them were fighting for the right to sleep in People's Park. After living for few months in a rent free house, she moved back to life on the streets.

During the Gulf War she took part in lots of demonstrations. When there were anti-war marches, she was always there.

In the Spring of 1991 she helped guard the Free Boxes and was active in the actions against plans to build a volleyball court and yuppify People's Park. During this time she'd been arrested for sleeping in People's Park, spare changing, and other minor charges. She helped organize an anti July 4th rally at the park and was there every night at the People's Park vigil. She also helped man a table for the Green Panthers. The cops knew her well. Her sarcastic wit bugged them, though her voice was usually gentle.

Some of the cops are O.K.
Some of the cops are scary as hell.
One of them handcuffed my friend and then stuck his hand in
her blouse and did more, much more.
He did that to some other women and it got reported but he's
still on the force.
Who decides who has the power?
I guess I wanted to show them how I felt.

Chapter Four

William Remembers

osebud was a writer. I've seen samples of her essay writing, and she was an excellent writer. She wrote great flyers too. Well, to digress a little bit, UC hired some allegedly homeless people to work on the pathways at People's Park. They weren't really homeless, it turns out. Most of them were crack heads. But anyway…she wrote this flyer entitled "Why Not To Work on the Pathways at People's Park". And it was, you know, a very articulate leaflet. I mean, detailed, and ran down all the reasons why you shouldn't work on the pathways.

What were you feeling when you heard of her death?
Surprise. A great deal of sadness. I was living up in Shasta County. The first time I heard about it was on KCBS radio. And the first report I heard the first day was that she was shot in the bedroom, rather that she was shot in the bathroom of The Chancellor's house. And the angle they were playing up was the fact that the cop had sustained, I think it was either three or five complaints, PRC complaints when he was a member of the Berkeley police.

The next day the story had an entirely different media spin on it. And also the whole circumstances had changed too. The second day the story had changed to—the cop was in the bathroom, and Rosebud was outside of the bathroom, which was a total flip-flop in the twenty-four hour period. And they were playing up the aspect of Rosebud's mental state when she was a teenager, I mean, earlier when she was, like, you know, twelve and stuff, rather than I think the nineteen that she was when she got murdered. And so I thought it was rather interesting that, within a twenty-four hour period, the facts of the case and the whole media spin put on it did such a flip-flop.

So I immediately started getting suspicious because I had talked with her and Andy, her boyfriend, about a week before the incident happened and she didn't appear depressed to me. In fact, I don't ever recall her appearing depressed. If she was, she certainly didn't show it to me. She always maintained a rather upbeat attitude, as far as I could tell.

So I was quite shocked at the reports of her death. And, like I said, the story did a flip-flop from the first day to the second day about her. First she's in the bathroom; the next the cop was in the bathroom. On the first day, you know, there's the cop who's trigger-happy because he's been shot himself by someone else, and the next day they're talking all this slander stuff about Rosebud. I immediately got suspicious, and I got down here, I think, the following Saturday after it happened, and started to talk to people about it. And the story just did not add up.

I actually believed the story that they were promulgating the first day, about how Rosebud was in the bathroom and the cop broke the door down in on her, and how he was trigger-happy because he had previously been shot five times in another incident, and how he had all those

PRC complaints sustained against him.

So the fact that he's had any complaints sustained against him is real significant because you've only got one chance in twenty of getting your complaint against Berkeley police for policeman's conduct, sustained.

The first thing that comes to my mind was early one morning. It was about maybe five o'clock in the morning.

It was during the Free Box trouble, when the UC police tore, I think it was like six or seven free boxes in a row a couple of years ago. And every time they'd tear down a Free Box, we'd just build another one, and every time they tore down a Free Box, people would bring twice as many clothes. Till eventually the whole park was just strewn with free clothes. You know, every time they'd tear down a Free Box it would make the news. So people would bring more clothes. In fact, there was an annex Free Box up the street. Anyway, I can't remember which Free Box it was—one of the later ones. I think it was maybe Free Box five or six.

I was there one night, guarding the Free Box, and it got down to maybe only one or two other people around. One of them was Rosebud. The cops came about five in the morning, and I asked the other person to go to the phone booth down at the corner of Telegraph and Haste to make a phone call, to call people and tell them, you know, "The cops are attacking the Free Box again."

And it was just me and Rosebud, and here's like, you know, uh, maybe a half dozen police cars, maybe a couple of dozen cops, a big garbage truck, and a whole bunch of heavy equipment and stuff to tear down this Free Box. And I'm thinking, "Well, OK. It's five in the morning.

There's only two people here. The third person, subsequently making the phone call, got arrested so he couldn't really do anything.

And then I went back up to the Free Box. And I told Rosebud, "Well, you know, it's five in the morning, and there's like three dozen cops here and just two of us. Let's get the hell out of here!" And she said, "Oh no. I wanna stay, you know, and see what's gonna happen." I didn't want to be there. I was just about to bug out. But I didn't feel cool bugging out and leaving her there by herself.

So I stuck around, though I was scared.

One of us had just been arrested, and there was like I said, maybe two or three dozen cop—UC cops, as opposed to like real cops —and me and Rosebud. But she said, "Oh, no. Let's not leave." You know, she didn't show the slightest bit of fear or anything. She may have been afraid, but she didn't show it. And that's just an instant which comes to my mind about her. So she was brave. Uh. You have to give her that.

As far as the fatal day, they obviously should have maybe shot in some tear gas, or just waited around, tried to starve her out, turn off all the utilities and electricity and everything, and just waited around. In fact, the University of California police has a book of rules and regulations which, of course, they totally ignored. In those rules and regulations they have specific guidelines for handling allegedly mentally disturbed persons. And those guidelines say, "Remain calm and try to wait the person out," which they clearly failed to do in this case. So I feel that they went in there with the intention of murdering her.

And I'm not gonna speculate on how she got in there or why because it can't help now.

Allegedly the Chancellor and his wife were in there at first, but once they were out safely, then there was no longer a threat—except to property, and we should value a life a lot more than property.

They used her breaking in as a justification in murdering her. I've lived in Berkeley for over fifteen years now, and I've seen a lot of wing nuts. I've seen enough wing nuts to where if I see one, I recognize them. And Rosebud was clearly not a wing nut. As I said earlier, she was very intelligent. And that's basically all I can say about that. I mean, she definitely was not crazy. Like I said, there are a lot of crazy people in Berkeley, so you've got a lot of things to compare with.

Cold-blooded, pre-meditated murder, like I said, is the word that comes to mind. That's all there is to it. They thought she was a threat to them.

Chapter Five
Everyone Remembers II

ight after the volleyball courts went into the park there were days of street fighting between People's Park defenders and assorted cops. Rosebud was arrested again for sleeping in the park. While she was there police found The Anarchist's Cookbook, firecrackers, chemicals and detonators at a campsite in the hills that they traced to her. So they charged Rosebud, Andrew, her boyfriend, and Timothy, with trying to make bombs. At the time these charges were filed, Rosebud was seventeen so she was sent to Juvenile Hall. She wasn't allowed visitors.

*That last night was like a vivid dream of how it had been
when they sent me to Juvenile Hall.
I'm always afraid of the dark.
Please don't let them send me to jail.
Juvenile Hall is jail.
I am in jail.
I am dead.
I'm seventeen and they have already killed me.
I'm seventeen and I'm dead.
Who killed me when I was twelve?
When I was six I died and the world hung by a thread of spit.
When I was six months old, before I grew up and crawled
back into the womb where I am now, I was joined to*

Emma Goldman at the hip like a Siamese twin.
I am an anarchist.
The first amendment is the one they break when they
arrest you for putting up a poster at a demonstration;
The second is the one they break when they caress you for
being female while they handcuff you and fail to read you
your rights.
The third is the tears they seek when they harass you for
huddling under an awning in the rain.
The fourth is the mistake they make when they think I
Rosebud, coming from an ancient line of warriors,
battered but still smiling, will take the bruising of
America anymore just lying down.

"It was this kind of thinking made me love her," say about nineteen street people and People's Park regulars simultaneously. Andy also, the one whose love she returned in the last weeks. Teddy who loved her too, and treasured her letters.

After two months they decided to try her as an adult. After she was returned to Santa Rita jail her bail was reduced to $10,000 and her friends posted the bond.

Once she was out of jail, Rosebud moved to the Info Cafe, a radical commune in North Oakland. She stayed active in the People's Park movement and she and Andy pitched a tent in People's Park Annex, a vacant lot formerly occupied by a burned out hotel. It had been taken over by homeless people a few weeks before.

The cops were always watching Rosebud. A month after she got out of Santa Rita she was re-arrested for resisting a police attack. Her friends again bailed her out.

She helped begin to build the People's Bathroom in the park, but cops ripped it up as soon as construction was begun.

When the Info Cafe had a problem in the spring of 1992 Rosebud and Andy moved to People's Park. They spent their days in the grove west of the driveway entrance. There were lots of homeless people who spent time there but University cops kept a close watch on the grove. They stopped there everyday, making arrests on small pretexts. During what was to be the last few days of her life Rosebud was almost constantly harassed by the police.

Dream or nightmare? I won't ever sleep. I was lying there worrying about the case when they shone their flashlights in my eyes. "Get moving, Denovo," they said. It wasn't a great night for trying to find a new place to sleep. Not many stars.

Chapter Six

Jim Henry Remembers

or a little while there I was uh, sort of her boyfriend. It's basically what I was itching to be all along. She had the sweetest smile, and the sweetest laugh. She had skin like velvet too—so soft and smooth. I loved touching it.

I'd said, "What is it about you that makes me want to do all this stuff for you?" She said, "Because I'm so cute, charming, and female."

She was all those things. I'm kind of new at all of this, so in the last couple of years I've learned quite a lot, and much of what I've learned, she taught me.

And we had solid political agreement. We were definitely pulling our oars in the same direction. She'd keep wondering if it was the fact that I was attracted to her that was making me agree with her politically, or whether I actually agreed with her, and I kept having to reassure her that, yeah, I was sincere in my political beliefs, and we did have actual political beliefs that were independent of any feelings that I might have had for her.

In everything she did, politics was very much in the upper part of her mind.

She was seventeen at the time, although I didn't know it. *When you just looked at the picture just now, you said how*

beautiful she was.
Yeah. She was.

When you first saw her, what ran through your mind–the very first time?
Uhhh. Let's see. I think I was just starting to come on to a hit of acid at that time. This guy that I'd met at this Fest in the City on Earth Day in '91, introduced me to her, and told me she was working on doing a rally for July Fourth. And I told her I was with Freedom Fighters which is another organization. It's been around longer that the Green Panthers. What they do is they go all across the country doing rallies. So she asked was I interested in co-sponsoring this event and working with her on it. And I said,"Sure." I figure, "Finally, my way in." And that's what it ultimately turned out to be.

This guy with the earpiece I was talking to at the Washington smoke-in back in 1980, I was asking him how could I get involved in all of that, and he goes, "Do the work. You'll get the recognition."

So for the last couple of years now, I've been doing the work and getting the recognition.

You knew the other people that were at the Info cafe?
Uhhh. Well, let's see. Mike L. was. This other guy named Jerry was. Unfortunately he's back in school in Ohio now. Otherwise I'd have him talk to you.

Did you ever see Rosebud cry?
Yeah.

What was that about?

I was never sure. Because it was like way late at night, and she just started crying and all I could do was hold her and try to comfort her. I kept trying to get her to tell me what was wrong, but she wouldn't. I guess there were just some things she wanted to keep to herself–keep private.

You felt she was in a lot of pain that last few weeks?

Uhhhh. Not really a lot of pain exactly. She had a lot on her mind, a lot going on.

Andy said she was really scared. She was scared of the two-year possible sentence hanging over her. That she was not, he said, a person who could be locked up. She had to be free.

Mmm. Yeah. She wouldn't have gotten along real well in prison. God! The way some of those tan bellies are in a prison... She'd of had all kinds of fun.

What's a tan belly?

OK. A blue belly wears blue, you know. Cops on the street, they wear blue. Uhhhh. Highway Patrol and pretty much all correction guards, uhh, they wear khaki. So they're tan bellies. Plain clothes cops are plaid bellies.

To what do you attribute... What do you think caused all this? Could something have been done by somebody else that could have avoided all that happened?

I kind of think the roots of all of this go clear back into her childhood. I don't know if there was anything really traumatic that occurred in her earlier childhood to make her so radical or if she was just so intelligent that she could see the truth behind all the government bullshit and she wanted to do something about it. I think that as long as we have an oppressive status system, an oppressive money economy, and people who are all too eager to tell other people how to live, we are going to get people who are so unwilling to put up with having their lives managed and regulated that they're prepared to make any sacrifice to re-establish freedom.

Well, that's saying society caused it. Just before you said that you felt that the roots of it went back to her childhood. Now let's assume that her parents loved her, (I have every indication to believe that's true). I asked Andy and he's not somebody who could be bullshit to. I'm sure her parents loved her, thought they were doing the best for her by obeying authority, thought they were helping. Beyond their control was a health care system that is about as fucked up as any other system in this country. And instead of it helping, unfortunately, it hurt. So let's stop blaming parents who were really doing the best that they could in every direction, even assuming that she was just a rebellious child who stood out in an upper middle class quiet academic kind of suburb. Even assuming that, I think we have to figure that when her parents thought they were getting her expert help, they were trapped in a system which is often harmful. And in this case, it was evidently was, because she came out feeling really traumatized, really bitter. And found it hard to readjust. They had done what they thought was right. They weren't being punitive. They were trying to help her.

Did Rosebud ever talk about having been in a psych unit,

and things that made her bitter about it?

She never really went into any detail about it. I'm trying to remember what little she did say.

What would be her main subject in conversation with her, when you were talking to her. What was there about her, apart from her looks, that drew you to her?

Oh. Her radical viewpoint. She was highly radical, politically. I really responded to that.

Where do you think that came from?

A lot of her reading, I'd say. She and I have read a lot of the same books. Like Orwell's 1984, Ira Loveman's This Perfect Day... She also read The Hitchhiker's Guide to the Galaxy Series. Umm. She's also read books by people I never heard of. There was one that was pretty much her bible, called Catechism of a Revolutionary. I've been sort of trying to find that, and it's a very rare book.

You've been spending just about every Saturday and Sunday trying to get a memorial to her cause. What are some of your experiences in terms of what people say to her? Do people stop and talk about her?

Sure A lot of people come up and ask what this whole archive is about, who was Rosebud, what happened? And when I explain to them about how she was murdered by the police, they show a lot of awareness and sympathy. Although some people have been a good deal less than pleasant. Some guy came up to me and said if she'd come into his house, he'd have shot her thirty or forty times.

Do you get many reactions like that?

No, that's been the only one like that so far. Some people kind of snort derisively as they go walking past. Most people, of course, don't even break stride to look at me. They think I'm just another panhandler, which I suppose I am.

But this is not for yourself. This is for a memorial purpose.
Mm-hm.

There was riot or a demonstration—I'm not sure what to call it. I was away when people in the Park, found out that she had been shot. I was told there was a demonstration which turned into a riot. Could you tell me something about that demonstration? Was there a riot? Were the police just calling it a riot? I get different answers from different people.

Well, there *was* a demonstration. We met in the Park. There were some speeches and then we moved to the Avenue.

Everybody, in a sense, has their own ideas. But I would really appreciate your fix on what happened afterwards.

You had told me that she telephoned you, but that the call was so brief and strange that you were almost...well, you were in shock. And you didn't know what to do actually, so you went into work, frightened because you had no way of communicating. The park friends had no beepers or phones to communicate with each other. What happened then?

What were the events of the day of her death, starting with the phone call that you received, and your reaction to it. And then, the later events of that day up to whoever organized the demonstration, going on through the demonstration. I think you would be telling something important because the events of that day were very critical to the supporters of the Park, people who agreed with what she was trying to do. There's been a lot of misinformation about it. I read in the media that there was a very violent demonstration, where stores were looted and cars put on fire and so on, by supporters of Rosebud. Is that true? But tell it, in sequence, starting from that morning. Starting literally from the phone call.

Yeah, that's not a day I'm likely to forget. But...I get up in the morning, get dressed, brush my teeth, shave, all of that. And I'm just ready to walk out the door when I get the phone call. So we go through the phone call—it takes about thirty seconds. And so, I go out my bedroom door, and my roommate's coming through the hall because she'd like to know who the hell's calling at six-thirty in the morning. And I tell her about the phone call, at least to the extent of saying that it was from Rosebud, and it was a very strange phone call.

What had Rosebud said to you?

She goes,"Hey, this is Rosebud. I called to say good-bye. I'm at The Chancellor's place. They're going to shoot me. Go tell the people in the Park." And that was it. Boom.

I was told later that about five minutes after we'd hung up, she called my roommate's son to ask if I'd left the house yet or not. He said,"Yeah." And she went, "Good." So it's like she thought I was on my way.

Could she have thought you were going to tell the people in the Park?

That's probably what she was intending. Yeah. The thinking part of my brain kind of shut down at that point. I seemed to be going on auto-pilot. So I went out, crawled into my bus, rode it into work, listening intently to the radio for any news reports. And as I'm going over the Bay Bridge (this is like a quarter to eight) that's when I hear the first word that there's been an incident on the Berkeley campus, and a woman's body been found. So I think, "Oh, shit!" because I know who's body that is…"

Then someone drove me over here to Berkeley, and that's when I joined in the demonstration. It was already going on about the time I arrived. There were people with mobile sound systems. People were giving speeches. Then we started marching onto the campus, yelling, "Murderers and assassins!" at the top of our lungs. "No justice—no peace!" "Fuck the police!" That sort of thing.

Then we had a little demonstration on the lawn in front of the campus cop shop. Then I heard that the police were looking for me because they wanted to talk to me about Rosebud's phone call. Somehow the rumor had gotten started that I had a tape of that conversation. But as I'm fairly allergic to being talked to by the police, I figured that was a good time to cut out and go home, which is what I did. So…I missed out on any subsequent events.

What happened during the demonstration? What was it like? Who had begun it? Or had it just spontaneously erupted here and there?

I think it was fairly spontaneous. The case of everybody saying, "Hey, let's go meet in the Park." So we met in the Park, and probably talked, and the sound system was gotten together, and people got up and started speaking, and matters simply progressed.

Did you feel pain that you hadn't been able to get in touch with the other people or go down there and try to talk to her through a loudspeaker? Andy felt if there had only been some way of all the friends getting there in time, maybe they could have persuaded the police to negotiate.

That probably would be true. Unfortunately, there simply was not time, because she was dead within half an hour of that phone call.

So, no matter what you had done it would have been to late. So they did not wait and try to contact people who knew her, to negotiate?

No. They could have called her lawyer. They could have called her parents. They wouldn't have been able to call me since I was out of touch with anybody then. But they could have called somebody! Shit! Their own hostage negotiation team, if nothing else. Except that Rosebud didn't have any hostages, so they probably figured it wasn't in their jurisdiction.

Some of your friends said that as soon as they knew it was Rosebud, they were not going to do anything helpful. They really wanted to get her because they were afraid she was a revolutionary.

Mm-hm. The police definitely had it in for her.

So to be a revolutionary now in 1993, what's that really mean?

To take your life into your own hands, is what it means.

During the demonstration did you see stores being looted or cars being burned?
No. All the images that I have that I saw on TV and that I've seen since, all seemed to have people just marching and cops pushing them back with billy sticks. I didn't see anything else. But in the media I read that all this other stuff happened. So I wondered which was true. Well, there's probably a certain element of truth to all of them. The media will, of course, try to put a spin on matters that are advantageous to the ruling class. You know, that is their function. To facilitate the authority of the ruling class.

Well, do you think there were stores looted that day, and if so, were the looters regulars of the Park, or people from other places who just came in and took advantage of the situation?
We began getting a lot of that last Summer. I recall there were some incidents right around Labor Day. Kids coming in from other parts of the East Bay, and generally going around crashing shit. The demonstration that I saw was peaceful. I have no way of knowing about what happened after I left except second hand.

OK So about what time did the demonstration end that day? Did it actually end or did it just kind of wind down?
Umm. Must have been around seven-thirty, maybe going on eight, by the time things started unwinding enough that I felt it was a good time to take off. Everybody else probably went back up into the Park.

What happened with you that night?

I got a couple of phone calls. One was from this one guy I've known for some years. I'd taken Rosebud over to meet him on one occasion last summer. And he invited me over to his place. I got together with him a week after she was killed, which was payday. So we sat around, toking up, and talking and we must have talked for a good couple of hours.

Did you talk about Rosebud?

Oh yeah. Definitely.

What were some of the things that were going on in your mind then?

I was just totally despondent. He could see that, the minute I walked in. He just saw waves of despondency shimmering away from me like heat waves on a asphalt top, you know. It was a rotten summer. I was very broken-hearted at that point.

Did you talk to any of your other friends about it?

A little bit. Not very much. I was ashamed of having fugued out when she called. I guess our individual wounds needed a little bit of time to heal. The next night I went over to this friend's house in San Francisco. Rosebud and I had gone over there on several occasions. And it kind of helped, talking to her, although I was pretty late getting home. It wasn't until that night that I was first able to start crying, that I come out of shock enough to cry.

What made you start a memorial archive?

Well, that got suggested to me by somebody else. Jonathan Montague —I'm not sure if you've met him yet

What happened then? Were there other kinds of protests or things being written? Did you connect up with anybody? That was the time that you left town, wasn't it, because you were kind of worried about being questioned by the cops.

No, I can't say I really left town, not at that point.

Then if you were there, what kinds of things were happening as a result of Rosebud's death?

Several things were happening .We did a rally for her on August 30th, Saturday. We had a rally at Haste and Telegraph, and my people were there. A lot of people got up and spoke. I got up also. At one point in my little speech, I reminded the cops of the Klingon proverb which states that revenge is a dish that is best served cold. But nobody actually took revenge. Andy got upset, I gather. When he hit the cop who was calling Rosebud names, he landed in jail immediately. He stayed there from August 25th to December 25th. So the most immediate result was Andy landing in jail.

Meantime, a columnist named Brenda Payton came out with a truly awful story. She's someone else who should be grateful I'm not into male violence against women. Otherwise you know…a little slapology . I wanted to shake up her head, and make it work better.

I think that was in the Oakland Tribune. Were any of the other newspapers into the same kind of thing?

They all made quite a bit about Rosebud's presumed mental instability, dysfunction, call it what you will. That was the basic theme they harped upon, that Rosebud was a mentally unstable person who should have been kept locked up in a psych ward the first time. All this media distortion in action.

Do you remember, Jim, any other particular incident when you were with Rosebud that was what you can call memorable in that something in your heart responded to what she was?

Mmm. Well, there was that whole first two-week period when I started hanging out with her so much.

What was she like?

Quiet, a lot of the time. Deep into her own thoughts.

When was that?

In June. Last two weeks of June.

Did anything change then? What was the pattern from June to August in terms of how it was for you?

Kind of up and down. Sometimes she'd hook back up with Andy and spend a lot of time with him. Then she'd break up with him and she'd be spending a lot of time with me. She never went to bed with me though.

If you met her parents tomorrow, if they came to Berkeley and you met them, would there be anything that you could say that could help them in any way? I feel for them. She may have been angry at them sometimes but most young people are angry at their parents sometimes.

I really don't know what I could say. I mean, their pain has got to be so much deeper than mine. I lost a friend. They lost a daughter. It's gotta cut a whole lot deeper. I don't know. Maybe I'd just give them a reassuring hug.

Now there is another mystery. I get different points of view from different people. Some people said that in 1990 when Rosebud first came, People's Park was peaceful enough that they could sleep there. They spoke of the time when they put up tents before the ten o'clock curfew. And that people were into helping each other. And it was more like a friendly sixties hippie commune. Then, when the curfew happened and the Free Box was first ripped out, all that other stuff started going down. Had you ever slept in the Park and not been hassled?

No.

It was Andy's contention and a couple of other people that I've spoken to that in 1990 it was relatively safe to sleep in the Grove in People's Park—that you could even put up tents if you wanted and people were helping each other.

Yeah, that's quite probably true.

And then, at the time of the curfew, all the hard drug dealing came in. I don't know. I just don't know. It seemed like Rosebud, a young girl who had been hurt, who had been raped, would not sleep in a place where she was afraid, and Andy's description of the Park in 1990 was that it was a safe place to sleep, especially if you had a tent.

Mm-hm

Then why did U.C. and the cops say that there was heavy dangerous drug-dealing going on, and therefore the park had to close at night?

Well, the only hard drug dealing I was ever saw was like in the mid-eighties. And between then and this one concert that I went to in October of 1990, I'd just never really gone up to the Park, so I didn't see any of that.

When was it that you decided on the plan of the memorial archives for Rosebud?

I don't know. February, March, something like that.

And part of that was making the garden in People's Park?

Yeah. Actually, that was Bob Sparks' idea, and I think it was a good one.

But I saw you really working at it, and Bob too. I saw everybody working at it.

Yeah. A lot of energy got put into it.

At one point, when the memorial was being planted on Earth Day, one of the people who was helping, took off his clothes and continued to work on the planting. What was your feeling about that?

I don't know – kinda casual indifference. If he wants to take his clothes off, let him take his clothes off. What the hell do I care?

Chapter Seven
Autopsy Part I

Autopsy performed upon the body of Rosebud Abigail Denote aka: Laura Marie Miller at the Coroner's bureau, 480 4th Street, Oakland, California, on August 25, 1992, at 10:25 a.m.

ANATOMICAL DIAGNOSES

1) MULTIPLE GUNSHOT WOUNDS
   A) ENTRANCES–NECK, TORSO, RIGHT HAND, LEFT HAND
   B) EXITS – TORSO
   C) BULLETS RECOVERED – TORSO
   D) PERFORATING DEFECTS – TRACHEA, CONNECTIVE TISSUE AND MUSCULATURE OF NECK, CONNECTIVE TISSUE AND MUSCULATURE OF TORSO, RIGHT PLEURAL CAVITY, RIGHT LUNG, PERICARDIAL SAC, HEART, LEFT PLEURAL CAVITY, RIBS, THORACIC VERTEBRAL COLUMN, SPINAL CORD, RIGHT HUMERUS, MUSCULATURE AND CONNECTIVE TISSUE OF LEFT HAND, PHALANX OF LEFT INDEX FINGER, MUSCULATURE AND CONNECTIVE TISSUE OF RIGHT HAND, PHALANGES OF RIGHT FIFTH FINGER

   E) BILATERAL HEMOTHORACES
   F) HEMOPERICARDIUM
2) VISCERAL ORGAN ISCHEMIA.

CAUSE OF DEATH: MULTIPLE GUNSHOT WOUNDS

EXTERNAL EXAMINATION

The body is that of a white female, appearing the stated age of 19 years There is a Coroner's identification tag present on the left big toe. The body is 63 inches long and weighs 107 pounds.

The body is presented in a supine position, with the head turned towards the right shoulder. Both arms lie alongside the body. The body is nude. Paper bags cover the distal aspect of each arm.

THE FOLLOWING ITEMS OF CLOTHING ARE PRESENTED WITH THE BODY AT THE TIME OF AUTOPSY EXAM: *(None of these items are present on the body.)*

1) A brown paper bag. Written on one side of it is the word "gloves" and written on the other side are the words "from hands". Examination of the contents of this bag reveals two rubber gloves. They appear to be partially turned inside out. In one glove there is a linear defect extending from the wrist outward to the finger area. In addition, on the same glove there is an open defect that has almost severed the index finger part of the glove from the remainder of the glove. This defect corresponds to an open defect on the index finger of

the left hand. On the other glove there is an open defect involving the fifth finger part measuring about 3/4 inch in greatest dimension close to the knuckle part of the glove. This corresponds to an open defect on the right hand. Both gloves are discolored with what appears to be blood. In addition, there are focal areas of yellow-brown discoloration of the gloves, most obvious in the finger areas. There is also some black discoloration in focal areas on both gloves, most obvious in the finger areas and to a certain extent on the palmar surfaces. (These gloves are not touched at the time of autopsy exam but are handled with forceps.)

2) Knee-length, blue Levi-type pants. They have been cut from the waist down both legs. No belt is present. There is an undone button and buttonhole at the waist in the front midline. These are intact at the time of autopsy exam as is also an open zipper. There is a scant amount of what is probably blood-staining of the pants. Some is present on the left lateral side in focal areas, roughly in the hip area. There is a scant amount present just below the right groin area. There is some vague black discoloration of the pants over the right front side and also down around the left knee and distal aspect of the left lower pant leg.

Present in the left front pocket is a square-shaped piece of material which is black with an extensive complex white design on it. This measures approximately 15 inches along each edge.

The two rear pockets are empty.

Attached to a belt loop (right front side, adjacent to the front button on the pants) by a piece of stainless steel wire (perhaps a paper clip) is a small black pouch with the word "Salem" written on it in green letters. In addition, on the front of the pouch is a digital-type clock and the time listed on the clock at the time of examination is 18:53. This pouch has a zipper over the top. Present inside the pouch is a square-shaped piece of bright pink silk-type material. it also appears to be a pouch of some type, although at the time of autopsy exam it is empty.

3) A pair of low-cut, lace-up, off-white Reebok shoes. The laces of both shoes are tied. The shoes are dirty and have focal areas of black material present on them.

4) A cut pair of off-white bikini-type underpants. They are tattered, especially about the waist area. There is a scant amount of red-brown discoloration in the crotch area.

5) A pair of white cotton socks. One sock has been either partially cut or torn from the superior ankle area roughly down to the heel area. Each sock has two red circumferentially oriented stripes about the ankle areas. Both socks are quite dirty. Worn, open defects are present in both heels. There is a scant amount of plant material present on the surface of one of the socks.

THERE IS BLOOD OVER THE FOLLOWING AREAS OF THE BODY:

1) Small amounts of blood present about the face. Much of this is present on the right side of the head which is adjacent to the autopsy table. There are scant amounts in focal areas lateral to the left side of the lips and the left side of the nose. There is a small amount involving

the left ear and the area between the left ear and the left orbital area.

2) Some blood present about the neck and upper chest, on the right anterior and left lateral sides of the chest, in the right clavicular area, manubrial area, and also over the anterior and superior aspects of the left shoulder.

3) Some dry and wet blood involves the posterior and lateral aspects of the right upper arm and also the posterior aspect of the forearm.

4) Some wet blood present over almost all of the back of the body.

5) Wet blood on the posterior aspect of the left arm, extending from the shoulder down to the elbow area. There is some dry, nonpatterned blood on the lateral aspect of the left upper arm. This extends from the shoulder down to the elbow area. The wet blood also extends down over the proximal one-third of the forearm, mostly on its posterior aspect.

6) Some dry, nonpatterned blood present over the right torso, extending from the axilla down to the hip area. From here a small amount extends down to the proximal one-half of the lateral and anterior aspects of the right thigh.

7) Some wet blood deposited on the body at the time of autopsy exam during removal of a sheet. There is an area present on the anterior medial aspect of the left thigh, occupying an area approximately 4 x 2 inches. There is also some spattered blood on the anterior medial aspect of the right thigh just superior to its midportion.

8) A small amount of blood in association with a gunshot wound on the left hand. This involves the dorsal aspect of the hand in the vicinity of the second and third knuckles. It extends out onto the second and third fingers.

9) a small amount of blood involving the nail area of the right fifth finger in association with a gunshot wound. Rigor mortis is not present. Lividity is nondiscernible.

THERE IS THE FOLLOWING EVIDENCE OF MEDICAL THERAPY:

1) A cardiac monitoring pad on the front side of the right shoulder.

2) A cardiac monitoring pad just below the left collarbone.

3) A cardiac monitoring pad just above the left costal margin.

4) A gauze-type dressing present over the left lateral side of the neck.

5) A plastic IV catheter in the left lateral side of the neck.

6) A tracheal tube entering into an apparent gunshot wound on the front side of the neck. The wound is on the anterior midline of the neck and from here it extends in a superior lateral direction over the right side of the neck. It measures approximately 2 inches in length.

7) A piece of yellow gauze lying on the lateral aspect of the left side of the body.

8) A hospital identification band present about the right wrist.

9) A plastic IV catheter in the lower right lateral side of the neck.

10) A plastic IV catheter in the left antecubital fossa.

11) A cutdown incision on the medial aspect of the right ankle.

12) A blood soaked piece of gauze superior to the left shoulder area.

Oral, vaginal, and rectal areas are examined grossly. Other than blood no fluid is identified about these orifices. No foreign objects are noted.

There is a 1/16 inch piece of metal on the skin of the right side of the face, approximately 1-1/4 inches posterior to the right orbital area. This is retained for evidence in a sealed envelope.

Prior to examination for blunt injuries of the skin, the scalp is shaven in the frontal area to expose an abrasion that will be described. It is noted at this time that the black material previously described on the skin of the face extends up onto the skin the scalp. The hair grossly exhibits no signs of singeing or burning. Likewise, the eyebrows and eyelashes are examined and no evidence of burning or singeing is grossly identified.

THERE ARE THE FOLLOWING BLUNT INJURIES TO THE BODY:

HEAD AND NECK

1) A 1/2 X 5/8 inch red-brown abrasion on the left forehead at the hairline and adjacent to the midline.

2) A 1/4 x 3/8 inch red-brown abrasion on the bridge of the nose.

3) A 3/8 inch red-brown curvilinear abrasion on the right side of the face, approximately 1-1/2 inches posterior to the chin.

4) A 3/8 inch V-shaped red-brown abrasion just superior and very slightly posterior to the previously described curvilinear abrasion.

RIGHT ARM

1) A 1 x 1/4 inch yellow-brown contusion on the posterior upper arm inferior to the midportion.

2) A 1/2 x 1/4 inch vague yellow-brown contusion on the posterior lateral upper arm, just slightly superior to the previously described injury.

3) A 1/4 x 1/4 inch vague green contusion on the anterior forearm just superior to its midportion.

4) A 3/8 x 1/8 inch partly green and partly brown contusion over the anterior lateral aspect of the forearm inferior to its midportion.

5) A 3/8 x 3/8 inch green contusion on the anterior medial forearm at its midportion.

6) A 1/2 x 1/4 inch gray contusion on the anterior lateral forearm inferior to the midportion.

LEFT ARM

1) A 5/8 x 1/8 inch red-brown abrasion on the medial proximal upper arm. The possibility of this representing a grazing gunshot wound cannot be ruled out. It is horizontally oriented, with the anterior end pointing superiorly at a 45° angle.

2) A 3/8 x 3/8 inch yellow-brown contusion over the medial elbow.

3) A 1/1/4 inch linear red-brown abrasion on the ante-

rior forearm, roughly midway between its midportion and the wrist.

4) A 3/8 x 3/8 inch red-purple contusion on the dorsal aspect of the index finger PIP joint.

RIGHT LEG

1) A 1/8 x 1/4 inch green contusion over the medial knee.

2) A 3/8 x 1/4 inch gray contusion over the anterior proximal lower leg.

3) A 1/8 x 1/8 inch vague gray contusion over the tibial tubercle.

4) A 1/2 x 3/8 inch vague gray contusion over the anterior lateral proximal lower leg.

5) A 1/4 x 1/4 inch vague brown contusion over the anterior lower leg, superior to its midportion.

6) A 1-1/4 x 1/2 inch yellow-green contusion on the lateral proximal thigh.

7) A 1/2 x 5/8 inch vague yellow-green contusion on the lateral thigh just inferior to the previously described injury.

LEFT LEG

1) A 1/8 x 1/8 inch gray contusion over the inferior border of the patella.

2) A 1/4 x 1/8 inch yellow-brown contusion over the tibial tubercle.

3) A 3/8 x 3/8 inch gray contusion on the lateral proximal thigh.

TORSO

No blunt injuries present.

The body is rolled to a prone position and further

examined. The black material on the posterior aspect of the neck is noted to extend superiorly into the scalp, involving the surface of the skin. Once again, no evidence of burning or singeing of the scalp is identified.

BODY MEASUREMENTS:

The distance from the sternal notch to the base of each foot is 50 inches.

The distance from the spinous process of the seventh cervical vertebral body to the base of each foot is 51 inches.

The distance from the most superior aspect of each shoulder to the base of its respective foot is 52-1/4 inches.

The length of each arm from the most superior aspect of the shoulder to the tip of the third finger is 27 inches.

THERE ARE THE FOLLOWING GUNSHOT WOUNDS PRESENT:

1) TYPE: Entrance.
LOCATION: Midline of the back, 2-7/8 inches inferior to the spinous process of the seventh cervical vertebral body.
SHAPE: Circular
SIZE: 1/2 inch in diameter.
ABRASION COLLAR: Present.
PRODUCTS OF COMBUSTION: None noted.
OTHER: Upon cleaning the body, some surface of the skin is focally scraped away, mostly on the left side of this gunshot wound.

2) TYPE: Entrance.

LOCATION: Posterior aspect of the right shoulder, 8 inches lateral and 3/4 inch superior to the spinous process of the seventh cervical vertebral body.

SHAPE: Circular.

SIZE: 7/16 inch in diameter.

ABRASION COLLAR: Present.

PRODUCTS OF COMBUSTION: Stippling is present in association with this gunshot wound. The stippling extends from the center of the gunshot wound posteriorly for a distance of 1-3/8 inches, superiorly for a distance of 1/3/4 inches, anteriorly for a distance of 1-1/2 inches, and inferiorly for a distance of 1-3/8 inches.

OTHER: There are at least three nevoid lesions on the lateral aspect of the proximal right upper arm. These are located approximately 4 inches from the gunshot wound. (They do not represent stippling.)

3) TYPE: Exit.

LOCATION: Posterior aspect of the right shoulder, 8 inches lateral and 2 inches inferior to the spinous process of the seventh cervical vertebral body.

SHAPE: Irregular. Re-approximating the edges gives it an irregular, roughly linear configuration.

SIZE: 7/8 x 1/8 inch

ABRASION COLLAR: Not present.

PRODUCTS OF COMBUSTION: None noted.

4) TYPE: Entrance.

LOCATION: Right anterior lateral side of the neck, 3-1/4 inches superior and 1 inch lateral to the sternal notch.

SHAPE: Roughly triangular.

SIZE: 1-3/4 x 3/4 inch.

ABRASION COLLAR: present, very prominent in the superior aspect of the gunshot wound, with the perforation being located at the extreme inferior end. The center of the perforation is located 3 inches superior and 3/8 inch lateral to the sternal notch.

PRODUCTS OF COMBUSTION: There is a scant amount of stippling in association with this gunshot wound. From the center of the perforation the stippling extends posteriorly for a distance of 2-1/8 inches, inferiorly for a distance of 1-1/4 inches, medially for a distance of 1 inch, and superiorly for a distance of 1 inch. Three stipple defects are prominent along the medial edge of the gunshot wound. In addition, there is a very prominent one inferior to it. At the time of autopsy exam no suture material is identified as being present in this area of the body.

OTHER: The long axis of this gunshot wound is oriented in a vertical direction, with the superior end pointing to the right at a 35° angle. The inferior edge of the gunshot wound is very irregular, and the possibility of some iatrogenic manipulation of this wound for placement of the tracheal tube cannot be ruled out. The tracheal tube is removed at this time. By palpation it is demonstrated to be properly located in the trachea.

(Over the chin area there are some vague nevoid lesions representing small skin tumors. These do not represent stippling.)

5) TYPE: Entrance.
LOCATION: Right front chest, 3/4 inch lateral and 1/2 inch inferior to the sternal notch.
SHAPE: Ovoid.
SIZE: 1-1/8 x 9/16 inch.
ABRASION COLLAR: Present. The perforation is located in the extreme lateral aspect of this gunshot wound.
PRODUCTS OF COMBUSTION: None noted.

6) TYPE: Exit.
LOCATION: Right front side of the chest, 1-1/2 inches lateral to the sternal notch.
SHAPE: Linear.
SIZE: 1 x 3/8 inch.
ABRASION COLLAR: Present.
PRODUCTS OF COMBUSTION: None noted.

7) TYPE: Grazing gunshot wound.
LOCATION: Lateral aspect of the left index finger, 23-1/2 inches inferior to the most superior aspect of the left shoulder.
SHAPE: Irregular.
SIZE: 2 X 1/2 inch.
ABRASION COLLAR: not identified.
PRODUCTS OF COMBUSTION: None noted.

8) TYPE: Grazing gunshot wound.
LOCATION: Anterior aspect of the right fifth finger, 23 inches inferior to the most superior aspect of the shoulder.
SHAPE: Irregular.
SIZE: 1-1/2 x 1/2 inch.

ABRASION COLLAR: There is a focal area of abrading along the distal aspect of this gunshot wound on its medial border measuring about 3/8 inch.

PRODUCTS OF COMBUSTION: None noted.

The hair is brown and about 14 inches long. Pupils are round. Irides are blue. Sclerae are white. No petechial hemorrhages are present. Ears, nose, and lips are without further abnormalities. The neck is without further abnormalities. No blunt injuries are identified. No ligature marks are noted. The chest is flat. Breasts are consistent with an adult female. The abdomen is flat. The external genitalia are nonremarkable and without evidence of injury. Legs and feet are without further abnormalities.

Chapter Eight

Andy Remembers

e had no place to sleep because of curfew. The curfew meant that you had to be out of the park by 10:00 PM. It got to the point where when people were demonstrating, it was guaranteed that cops would come and try to break in, and run everybody off. We'd be marching down the streets and they'd come with their cars and jump out and just start chasing people all over the fucking place with night sticks and guns and we'd break up like birds and then we'd relocate somewhere else and continue on.

How did you meet Rosebud?

We had some friends who were talking about going out on an action because the streets become ours at night. The police do chase us all over and try to keep us from demonstrating all day. So we tended to express ourselves in the middle of the night artistically. Rosebud and a friend of mine were discussing decorating a police car and she started laughing and wanted to come with us to help us decorate this police car. We had things like spray paint and well, other implements of decoration.

We never did do that, of course. We couldn't do anything like that it was too dangerous, but when we were discussing it, we knew we talked the same language. So we just started hanging out together, and we liked each other a lot.

You know the difference between a cop car and an elephant? An elephant has its trunk in the front and its asshole in the back. Actually that's a joke Rosebud liked. The first time she bailed me out of jail, I'd heard that one in jail, and I told it to her.

I'd been jailed for doing some property damage to a building during a demonstration. And she got me out—saved me.

Sometimes it was like living with a bird, you know, some kind of singing bird...She was a really good writer. She was a poet. She used to like making flyers too. They were very concise. She was very good at communicating cordially with people. When she worked a fourth of July smoke-in, about three or four hundred people showed up. We were all a non-nuclear bunch in the middle of the park listening to music. The police were staring at us.

She was very intelligent and there were a lot of activists around here already good at organizing. And I think what she did was just watch somebody do something and just started doing it herself. You know...she'd carefully observe. Things that worked she would use; things that wouldn't, she would drop.

The happiest day I ever had with her...God, there were so many. We had some really good days. We also had some rough ones. Sometimes we were very very good at loving each other. And sometimes we were, just well, lousy at it. We were getting physical. That's the way we got along, you know. Sometimes it wasn't a very graceful relationship.

She was a soldier. She was a warrior. She was five foot nothing, man. She's the damsel who went out to the fucking grave.

I saw her about eight hours before she was shot. We were talking to each other. She didn't tell any of us at all what she had in mind. We just didn't know. Nobody knew until she called Jim, I think. When she called him to talk to him she must have tried to get us up there to help her. That was the message that I heard her get out, that I was told she said. Jim Henry feels bad and guilty that he didn't do anything when she called. He said it happened so fast, that she hung up so fast that afterwards he kept saying, "Could I have done something?" But he didn't. He wasn't able to.

I think as a movement we are not able to respond quickly enough to any emergency like this. They've got an edge on us, that they use to help keep us from our rights, and it is that they are a bunch of paid flunkies who are, can be depended upon to act in certain ways, given any certain stimulus. In other words, they knew what was happening, and they were there – guns, dogs, tasers, fuckin' tear gas and all that shit. And they killed her. We weren't ready to respond. We could have been there too. And now I'm nowhere, man. I would have done anything it would have taken to get her out of there, but we didn't know. And well, you know, Jim was confused probably, and shocked when he got that call.

Well, he was paralyzed to do anything. He said he would let everybody know. Maybe she thought she would get backup by calling. Instead he rode into San Francisco on the bus, and I guess he got paralyzed.

Before he even got there he heard on a portable radio of her death. She had asked him to tell her people at the Park.

That's where all us warriors are.

He didn't.

She had no help. If there had been a big protest right outside they might have just afraid to do what they did.

We could have responded in so many ways. What we could have done is just got a bunch of anarchists up there and yes, as far as the cops, got in their faces, and made them do the right thing. And if they didn't we could have fought them, and gotten her out alive. We could have done it either way. But we weren't there.

That's one problem I've got with it. . . as far as communications go I want walkie-talkies. Shit like that. Because your brother or sister might go off like that. and we might have to rescue them from these beasts.

She was right. That person who shot her was an enemy. He was an enemy to everybody who is poor. He was an enemy to everybody of color. He was an enemy to us all. He was an enemy even to this college. He wants to turn it into another party college. With plenty of money for basketball and shit. He's wanting to wage war on homeless people. That's why she went in there. She felt we had to do something. Otherwise we're dead, hopeless.

So what she did then, you feel was a classic revolutionary act?
Yes, she was a soldier.

Do you think the newspaper reports about her being emo-

*tionally disturbed and so on, were just to excuse what hap-
pened in the house?*

For hundreds of years in many countries, the powers
that be have labeled people who did not go with their little program —"mentally disabled." They put us in any
kind of institution they've got room in because we're a
danger to them. That's why. They've done this. They still
do it all the time.

I have a friend. I met a dude in jail. He was a psychiatrist, and he worked in Ireland. And he used to do that
regularly, just walk, insulting our mental institutions.

And what he would do, he would help the IRA to rescue the people in locked wards. He told them where they
were going to be and helped get them out. He was really
cool. He probably kept me from killing myself—you
know. He was cool. He'd got three of his fingers blown
off with a stick of dynamite when he was younger.

*A 90 year old activist who I've been documenting landed in
jail for 22 months for stopping evictions in the 1920's. He
would stand there along with the people being evicted, and the
marshall would put the furniture out on the sidewalk. He'd
just stand there and put it back in. They called it obstructing
justice. I call it "obstructing injustice."*

Yeah. That's what it is. "No, I don't want to leave my
home. Thank you very much. I think I'll put my stuff
back, you know." A lot of us who see that are now in the
movement—we cut locks off buildings and move in

*There's the old Montgomery Ward building in Oakland,
and it could have a thousand studio apartments. It's been*

empty for almost nine years, so we're all trying to get the city of Oakland to take it over. But those legal ways take years and years.

I know, that's part of the thing with Rosebud. She had no patience with that. Endless, endless years.

She was very involved with squats for the homeless, but she didn't have a lot of faith in whether it would work or not because — well — they own the courts, you know. And we both knew it, but we still worked on it. We worked on it all kinds of legal ways — not so much to win, at least to obstruct them because their justice system is completely screwed. It's like it's set up to keep change from occurring. It's set up to keep the same people in power. She knew it; I knew it. Anybody with a brain knows that.

Then Rosebud was a classic revolutionary?
Yep, she sure was.

And in the tradition of Joan of Arc?
Yeah. I don't know. I think Joan of Arc actually worked for like the king or queen at the time that she got burned up at the stake.

And God...
Yeah, yeah, Joan of Arc worked for God. But Rosebud was an atheist. She was a dedicated atheist anarchist warrior. I don't know that much about Joan of Arc. She might have been all that stuff.

I guess there's no way of knowing. The last time that you

saw Rosebud, what do you think was going on in her mind?

The last time I saw her was like eight hours before this happened. It was two or three in the morning when we parted company. The only clue, (which wasn't much of a clue) was that she wanted to spend some time by herself. And I didn't think much about it. We did that all the time.

I mean, we loved each other, but we'd get into arguments. We wouldn't even talk to each other for two weeks at a stretch. You know, we'd just be really pissed. We'd get back together though. Like all she said was she wanted to just have some time alone, some space.

When I started thinking about who killed Rosebud, I came to the conclusion that *everybody* did, you know.

I know exactly what you mean. Everybody! We've all got a piece of this to share. Her pain went back a long time before you'd even met her, probably.

Well...this world killed her. The locked psych units, maybe the schools, the whole bit. Her parents probably regret having sent her to a psych unit. They thought that it would help.

Everybody in this world has got a piece of her death on his shoulder, just like we do so many others who grew up that way. There are a lot of people who die in their spirit just because we're not very able to treat each other correctly. We're not mature. We're insane as a race, as a species. And until things like governments, jails and prisons and all that stuff is gone, we're not gonna make it.

Right now, while I speak to you, they are stripping some rain forest somewhere — completely ignorant of the fact, seemingly, that that was what makes our air. They're dumping garbage in our oceans. They're jailing people for protesting a situation they're creating, for going out and trying to change this place, for being troubled, for being different.

They executed her. That was pre-meditated murder. They're gonna cream me, I've got a feeling. I don't have room to move or breathe sometimes anymore, it seems. Those fucking pigs are on my ass like stink on shit, man. So I know how she felt – exactly how she felt. I know that if this keeps up, I don't know how I'm going to act.

But I believe I've had enough. I'm tired of being abused. I'm tired of being fucked with. I'm tired of their killing my friends. I'm tired of this shit. These people. They're vultures.

Her anger probably started a long time ago. Way before she got to Berkeley.

Oh sure. She's been mad about the way things are for a long time. See, she was a very intelligent girl, and she did not have any problem figuring out what was right and what was wrong. And she'd been pushed around. She'd been raped once. She'd been abused by this world for two reasons, well three.

Because she was small, she was female, and she was an anarchist. And she wasn't somebody who just spouted, you know, something she'd read. She had a mind of her own. She understood how bankrupt all these other political philosophies and ways of thinking are because we're failing at it.

I think what you're saying is it's not only who killed Rosebud, it's also what killed Rosebud. And what's still going on.

Well, what the cop did – I hate him and all he stands for. And, well, he's just a tool, a poor pathetic puppet who went in there, because he got paid to go in there.

Now he's got blood all over his fucking hands. He's a real piece of shit. To allow yourself to be used as the tool of execution for a five-foot tall girl. She was 19 years old! And that cop had a night stick. He had a fucking trained dog, and mace and a taser.

What's a taser?

It's a shock pistol. They point it at you, and it delivers, you know, voltage to just like put you on the ground. It's part of the new high-tech crowd control experimental equipment they've got. At least that's my understanding of the situation.

Didn't Jim Henry say she was so little, he could've taken her out with a baton stick?

He could've. But I knew Rosebud. And I'm thinking, if he did take her out with a night stick, he'd probably have to beat her down like Rodney King because that girl was not going peacefully. But, for instance, if he'd used mace, there wouldn't have been a thing she could have done. Or if he'd used his taser he could have stunned her.

What was he doing in the fucking room anyway? Why didn't they say, "Look, the house is surrounded. You ain't coming out of there." They could've tear-gassed the place if it came right down to it. And they didn't even need to be in that building. It's like they decided to play this weird, poisonous game of hide-and-seek, and just throw away all the accepted methods of getting people out of situations...

Yes, they just threw them away. They said, "This is Rosebud. Let's kill her." That's what they did.

Carol said if it was three fraternity brothers breaking and entering, they would have used negotiations.
Yeah. They would've.

The house was empty?
Empty. There was nobody in there, except her. You know the funny thing about this is none of us anarchists are getting paid for what we do – for trying to make these changes in society. And I'll tell you what. If you took those cops and you cut off their paychecks, they wouldn't even have been capable of that act. That cop wouldn't have been able to do it. He did it for fucking money. He killed her for money. They hired him, and so he absolutely mother-fucking went in and did it.

What was it like the week or two before? People say different things. Some people say she was depressed. Some people say she wasn't depressed.
I think she might very well have been depressed.

Why? Apart from what's happening in the whole society? Anything personal, apart from that? Yukon Hannibal said it was because in the movement itself, people were just talking. There was a lull in terms of action.

Like I said before, we'd get into fights sometimes, being mad at each other for two or three weeks at a time and we were just coming down off one of these jags. That was the first time I'd talked to her in two weeks. It was weird because we were getting along really well that night. We were treating each other like human beings. And then she did this.

So this had to be a political act, not just a personal act, because personally, you had made up?

It was a combination of everything. We hadn't really made up, but we were treating each other very decently. We were friends again. But people aren't that simple. Nothing is just a political act, or nothing is just a crime of passion. Nothing is that simple. Things combine. People react. Especially people like her.

She had lost hope. She was facing going to prison on charges of possession of a destructive device – things of this nature. I was being charged for the exact same thing. And she was scared. She was really frightened. She did not want to go. That was one thing that she couldn't bear. They were talking about giving her like two years. For her that would have been an eternity because she was a creature that had to have its freedom. She was not going to be put in a cage.

She'd get in demonstrations on the street, and that woman put up a fight. She was not getting in cop cars without being physically forced. And that meant using every means at her physical disposal. Luckily she was only five foot tall. Otherwise she might not have even lasted as long as she did. But, she meant it. She wasn't fucking around when she said she wanted to be free. She wanted to go to demonstrations and say whatever she had to say. She wanted to make a change. And they were trying to keep that from her. You could not take her peacefully. She would have to fight. Sometimes I understood her and sometimes I didn't. I think the next time they arrest me, I'll fight because I'm just worn out.

And all these times that you've been arrested it's been for things that were connected with changing the society?
Yeah. I'd never been arrested before on anything like drug charges or any of that shit.

So it's really about changing the society. It's about revolution.
This isn't some party. This is the real deal. The reason we're here, in this town at this point in time is because there's a lot of people like us. Northern California's flaky, and anarchists can be too. But they all understand that we need to be free. And they all come here because this is where we all are. A lot of of us. There's a few free people all over. But there's a lot of us here. We're an actual society here.

The free speech movement started in the Sixties here, and that's what the Park is all about. And that's what Rosebud was all about, I guess. Where did you come from, Andy?
Well, I'm from New Mexico and Arizona. That whole desert down there all the way from Death Valley. We were in New Mexico. We kind of peppered all over that desert.

So you're from a freer place, actually.

Comparatively speaking, yeah..

Was there any particular time that you and Rosebud had a quarrel over politics?

That was mostly what our differences were. Some of the quarrels were personal. But it was very rare. Usually it was something like "Should we nuke Lexington, Kentucky or not?"

You spoke of her parents. Of course they felt horrible. But was there anything they say that would put some light on what happened?...

No, they haven't said anything as to why. I haven't talked to her father. But I have gotten a letter from him and I've written him a couple of times. Interestingly enough, the first time I tried to write him, my letter just disappeared in the U.S. mail. And I'm not stupid. I know how to address a letter. I made sure I put a stamp on it. And the damn thing just went pff... Actually it was a tape I made for him.

Well, if you make another, send it registered and they can't mess with that. That's a Federal offense if they mess with registered or certified mail.

They murdered Rosebud. I don't think they'd balk at messing with the mail.

We set up a mailing address that nobody else knows but me, so I can get letters now. You know, a lot of the people in this movement miss Rosebud. We've got a bunch of separatists trying to work together as a unit and it's not working. We've got to put aside our bullshit, and try to recognize that we've all got a thing we've gotta do.

For instance, I've seen heterosexual homophobes hating homosexual heterophobes, black people putting down white people, Asians putting down Latinos. The whole riff, all the dumb shit. It doesn't have to be like that—most of the people in the movement who have anything to do with this, they need to get their heads out of their asses and just start working together towards goals.

Or it's like wasting each others time trying to do the same things that the system's doing. See, Rosebud and me, this was one thing we discussed a lot. That's why we'd stand around and finally say, 'Let's get it together and go kick their asses.' You know. we're not going to get it done by fucking around the way we have been . We're getting badly hurt right now. And we're gonna continue getting hurt until we finally learn how to move.

Do you feel the most important thing now is to try to get a group of survivors together instead of everyone just doing things separately?

Well, it's not so much a matter of even doing things separately. It's a matter of letting people do the things they've got to do, and not giving people a hard time about whatever it is they decide they have to do. A lot of times propagandists really piss me off because, you know, flyers and stuff are well and good, but they've got their place. There's other things we need to do also to make a difference in this mess.

So how do we remember Rosebud?
By still trying to fix the things she tried to fix.

Chapter Nine
Everyone Remembers III

Months later Jim Henry, remembering shock, said "My brain turned off. I just went into an automatic mode. I didn't think there was anything I could do so I just rode the bus into my job as a dishwasher in the city. After Jim learned from his roommate's son that Rosebud had called again but he'd already left. The "If I only had done this or that" blues began to attach themselves to him and everyone left alive.

What killed Rosebud, beside the paranoid police officer they sent in with his police dog, his tear gas, his taser, his mace, his billy stick? We had begun unintentionally killing Rosebud from the time the authorities' advice was taken and she was sent at twelve to the psych ward that was, like many psych wards, a unique system of dictatorship, to the moment the four bullets were fired. Two entered her chest, two her back. The trajectory of the bullets, as shown at autopsy months later, were down, contrary to the first information the media was given. Who and what killed Rosebud, we were all later to learn, was that all of us did.

Our sweet beautiful daughter. Are we then responsible for your death?

Should we have just called you a rebel with a cause, and not listened to their diagnosis, right out of some manual of behav-

ior that defined conformity as normal?

When you were a warrior, I was a worrier. Daddy was too. We did what we thought was right.

I love you, Rosebud.
I love you too, Andy.
I'll always love you, little warrior, even though you and I have our political differences.
We do have our political differences.
Never mind. Let's just turn in and get some sleep.
Andy, I need some space tonight. I need to be alone for a while.

So, seeing this statement as just like ones he had heard before, knowing no "competitors" were lurking in the shadows, Andy left. He didn't know that the cops were going to barge in, making her move, with no place to go.

Oh lost and by the wind grieved Thomas Wolfe, come home again! Rosebud where shall you roam? How shall you wander home?

They said that when Rosebud's entrance into the Chancellor's mansion later, tripped a silent alarm, the UC police came and got the Chancellor and his wife out.

So the house was empty.

Anyhow they say that Rosebud was spotted by a cop through a window who ordered her to drop her weapons. The cop recognized her from before. The UC police then brought in a K9 unit from the Oakland Police Department to find and capture her.

Chapter Ten
Burke Remembers

 got mad when a cop insulted
Rosebud and I hit him
and went to jail.

Did they keep you?
Just overnight. I got out the next day.

That's good. They kept Andy for six months, from August until Christmas. So he was very bitter. They said it was assault. It was like what happened to you — a cop was insulting her. You went to high school with Rosebud. Do you know anything about the situation that sent her to a hospital?

Not really. I know that we went to a pretty upper middle-class Catholic high school. From what she said then it seemed like her parents sent her there to try to, you know, straighten her out, or whatever. That they wanted to, you know, fix her up, or whatever. I remember her always, you know, smiling and she would do stuff at school just to do it, you know, to mess up the system, really. Most of the other people at the school we went to were just – they didn't know what to think of her. They pretty much kept away from her. They thought she was way too out for them, or whatever. They were a pretty straight bunch.

So she was a rebel, then, almost from the beginning?
From when I knew her.

What year in high school?
I remember when she started sophomore year, and I had homeroom with her. And I think one other class that year. I would see her in the halls all our sophomore year and then part of our junior year, and then we had a science class: anatomy class together.

That hospital that she went to, I knew a lot of other kids who were sent there, and for a while when I was growing up I was scared that I was gonna get sent there, too. And, uh, I don't know, I heard a lot of bad stories about the place.

I'm not sure what the exact years were that she was in there. I know she was there before I met her at high school. What it probably did was make her more rebellious than she had been before. I don't think that she was there very long. Just a few months. I'm not sure how long. I know her parents regret that a lot. You know, some shrink says do this, do that. People get scared, they think that the shrinks are the experts so they know what to do.

Right. Do you have any particular memories of her? Any special day that something happened, or you were with her or, just about any feelings that you had about her when you were both in high school, before going to Berkeley?
Well, for some reason I really remember the first day we had homeroom together and the first thing she said was that although the teacher called her Laura Miller, her real name was "Rosebud." And everybody was just kinda

like, "okay," you know. They didn't know really what to think. She used to just do things that, things that nobody at that school could figure out. It was funny. Like she would just carry all her things around in a box instead of putting them in a locker. She was really smart. And she would do things, like when we would have to take standardized tests she would try to purposely get everything wrong on them while everybody else was trying to do their best. In high school she tried to get things started in the city of Lexington. She wrote a long, long street theatre piece and tried to get a lot of people involved. Like anyone in school. She asked everybody she kind of knew to be in this – it was very political – street theatre. She tried to organize an anarchist gathering to be held at a library one time, but the library didn't really like that. They wouldn't let her have any space.

She was an anarchist before she came to Berkeley, then?
I don't know. At the time I really didn't know anything about anarchism at all. I was wondering what she was doing. She tried to get a public space at the library to organize anarchist things.

Was it her reading that got her started on anarchism? There wouldn't have been much going on there in Lexington.
I guess it must've been that. Lexington's a pretty apathetic town.

All I really know about Lexington is that people went there to get off heroin, that there was some kind of federal hospital? Don't they have the Rockefeller program?

I don't know.

People I knew said it was pretty awful. You know, of all the people I talked to Burke, you're the one who knew her first. Maybe not best, maybe Andy knew her best.
Probably.

You knew her before she came to Berkeley. From the things I heard, she became more and more depressed those last few weeks. The cops kept hunting up where she was sleeping, and threatened her almost continuously.

So more and more pain and anger. But I think that must've started a long time before. For her to have become an anarchist says that she felt that the system, as it existed, was pretty lousy and that she was looking for solutions.

Of course that doesn't make her crazy. It's very hard to find any clue from anybody that she acted, you know, crazy. Most people say she never really acted crazy. When you said the kids felt it was strange that she always carried all her things around, since this was after she had been in the hospital, that might have been a very logical reaction to psych units where people often lose their possessions. Other people who are really sick either steal them or destroy them. So she might have just felt the need to hang on to her stuff.

One story that I remember is that, well I wouldn't call it crazy but uh, some people at the school did. We had to do reports about saints. We had a religion class since it was a Catholic school. And she made up her own saint called Ronald McSexburger. She said he was her patron saint. They did the reports in a chapel, and presented them, and she had a really religious teacher who was sensitive about things like that. So it probably upset the teacher a whole lot. And she opened up a Big Mac wrapper and unfurled a condom, which, you know, at a Catholic school causes a lot of problems. Within an hour the whole school knew about it. She did things like that.

So she never really wanted to be accepted by the straight world. It seems like she was doing everything to rile them.

Right. It didn't seem like she wanted to be accepted by the school at all, as far as I could see. Once she came to Berkeley, she dropped out of school. Before, she'd also dropped out of school and then tried to go to college in Kentucky, but that didn't work out. After she came out here she'd call me periodically and it was a surprise every time because I wouldn't expect it at all and I wouldn't ever have any way to get in touch with her. I don't know. She seemed really excited about being out here. But it was always kind of strange that she'd call me because we weren't really close in school. We just kinda knew each other a little bit. Maybe she wanted somebody to talk to back in Kentucky about what was going on here. I don't know.

Maybe she sensed that you weren't condemning her like the straight ones, and maybe – was she trying to persuade you to come out here?

I don't ever remember her saying anything like that.

Did she indicate that she was suffering when she was here?

She said at some point that she was staying with some people that were of a different political. group. Leninists or Communists or something. I don't remember exactly. And she was worried that they would find out that she was more of an anarchist and kick her out. But other than that, she seemed all right I guess. I just remember her calling me, you know, quite a few times. The first time I came out here by myself it didn't even occur to me that she was out here or still might be here. I was living in San Francisco for a little while, and it didn't occur to me that she would still be here until I saw her picture on the front page of the paper.

So you actually didn't connect with her before the incident? That must have been one hell of a shock.
It was – completely. I'd been squatting in San Francisco and didn't really come over to Berkeley very much. For some reason she had slipped to the back of my mind. I didn't really even think 'Rosebud's been in Berkeley for a while. She's probably still there,' until I saw her picture in the paper when I was walking down the street.

She died August 25, '92. When had you come out to California?
I guess I had gotten to San Francisco in the middle of July, and then had been in the city that entire time, pretty much.

So you'd been there only a month.
I probably would've come over to Berkeley eventually and run into her.

Did she ever talk about the hospital or why she had been sent?
Not really. It was just a place that parents who think

they have really wild kids, send them. That's what it always seemed to me.

Everybody that I've spoken to said how bright she was. How smart and well-read. Had she talked about any ideas with you? Had she tried to convert you to being an anarchist?

Well, like I said, she wrote a really political play. It involved the Pope, George Bush and Dan Quayle. People who were in power at the time. And a lot of...different wide reaching things that made me think. At the time I was sheltered. I had an idea about some things, but her play made me think a lot more. I don't know that I remember us having any just straightforward political conversations. We would talk about environmental things, about how the world was just getting destroyed. That was my main focus at the time, so that was something we could connect on.

You both were from regular middle class families? Did you ever go to where she lived?

No, I rarely saw her outside of school. I would run into her sometimes but mainly I talked to her at class or in the hallways. And sometimes at lunch.

When you came back to Kentucky after San Francisco, did you ever see her parents or talk to them afterwards?

I never did. For a long time I wanted to go see her grave and thought the only way I could find out where it was would be to ask her parents. But I felt kind of weird. I didn't know how they'd react to me saying I was a friend, so I never did call. And then I talked to someone else who knew you could just go to the cemetery and ask.

Which cemetery?
Lexington Cemetery on Main Street in Lexington. I never did talk to her parents. I just went to the cemetery. I found out where she was buried in March or April and the person I talked to there remembered her – remembered the family. I said, "Laura Miller, her given name," and he was like, "oh-oh, yes. I remember the family, and remember her."

Her lawyer had wanted to bring a lawsuit against the Oakland Police Department but her parents decided against it. I guess they were trying to get away from the pain, not bring it up all over again. So that's pretty understandable. I think they suffered a lot feeling they had made the wrong decision obeying authorities and shrinks, sending her to that hospital. I'm sure they meant well but probably any hospital like that is just the wrong place to send a kid like that.
One thing I heard from some other people, or maybe I read it somewhere after she died, but they said she attacked the principal of the last school that she went to. I'm not sure if that was just a rumor. I'm not sure how truthful it was.

I had read that, too. If they say somebody's violent and a minor, parents can have them committed.
That might've had a good deal to do with it.

Would that have been the same high school or a different one?
No, that was the public high school, before she went to

the Catholic High School.

What was the name of the high school you both went to?
Lexington Catholic High School.

Chapter Eleven
Yukon Remembers

My name is Yukon Hannibal and, um, I've known Rosebud ever since she arrived here in Berkeley. When I first met Rosebud it was right here, you know, in a situation like this food line. She looked so young, unlike lots of the people in the park at the time. Of course, there were other young people, but it was something different about Rosebud, you know. She would be in line, she'd get her food, she'd eat her food, and then she would run back and forth through the park, you know, like—she was running towards something, or running away from something. I'm sure it was just her spirit to get out that extra energy that was in her body. So we got to talking, you know. I found her a very pleasant person. Extremely articulate and very revolutionary minded. I was amazed, you know, because I've been a revolutionary my whole life, you know. I've been with—I've struggled with a lot of, you know, revolutionary groups in the past, you know. And here's someone so young, so fresh and so white, and she was involved with the revolution. Yeah, it kinda blew my mind, you know. So I kinda touched with her, philosophically, you know, I, uh, probed into her, you know, to really try to pick out her views and see if they were similar to mine. They were. But Rosebud was very vocal about her opposition, just like I am, you know. I had a People's Park paper route there and I would start throwing literature and put it out there and Rosebud would come and help me. When the police would harass me... she would be there, you know, I mean, she'd be there, right there by my side, you know, and sayin', " Hey, that's my friend. Leave him alone." And she was always there, you know, for me. She was out there in front of Cody's doing her table, you know. And I was there for her. I used to sit and help her carry her table to the spot where she'd set it down.

I met Rosebud one day and we talked. We went down to this park and we had a very long conversation about God. She had absolutely no belief in God, you know, so I kind of told her: "Well, I'm really afraid for you." I said, "There's something that's going on inside of you that you're not revealing to me or anyone else." She said, " We can't talk about it." And she got extremely upset, you know, and she started accusing me of wanting to have sex with her, and I said, "No, that's not the situation, you know, I just wanna make sure that you don't do anything foolish that would get you, uh, killed." And, uh, she needed a blanket that night, you know, 'cause she was crashing up in the hills. Her and her boyfriend was fighting, and they wasn't on good terms at that time. And so I went, uh, to this house, Set Free House, which is a Christian house, and I got her my sleeping bag, you know. And I asked people, you know, from my groups (you know, the spiritual group and the revolutionary groups) to pray for Rosebud and try to keep her out of harm's way. I spoke my feelings to many people in the movement, and, uh, I had a dreadful feeling that something was gonna happen. I was away for two weeks and I was there, and when I came back I was informed of the Rosebud assassination. When that hit me, I was devastated. But I wasn't surprised, because I kinda felt in my heart that something was terribly wrong. Her loss to me, you know, was tragic—she was my sister, and I loved her very much. The fact was we both protected each other, we both struggled together, we organized the people together. And she was a great revolutionary sister. That she went out the way she did—I was hoping that if she'd do something like that she would at least do it in the company of others. I don't know. I feel guilty for going away then 'cause I know if I was here, she'd probably be alive today, you know. But I had to go for my own well-being, you see, because I was really low on my tolerance level at the time. 'Cause I'd been on the streets a year and a half, you know, I helped create the People's Park Annex, you know, before the fence went up. I helped organize the sleep-ins and the protests on the side of the park. So at that last stage of the struggle I kinda needed to get away and become spiritually cleansed. I had asked Rosebud to come with me and she was about to come until I told her I was going to a spiritual retreat. She didn't want nothing to do with that so, you know.

How do you think they should've handled it?
Of course, they knew it was Rosebud, even though her hair was dyed, they knew instantly who she was, and I think that precipitated the assassination. Now had it been anyone else, like just a person from the college, or any other person other than Rosebud, they would've used

other tactics. There was nobody in the house for her to harm. It was murder. Just straight forward murder, you know. And someday it's gonna cave in on them, you know. 'Cause people like me, people like Bob Sparks and David Nadel and Jim Henry and Carrol and other soldiers of revolution won't ever let 'em forget Rosebud, you know.

Other people who knew her all said the same thing.

See I feel that Rosebud was brilliant. Her situation, like most homeless people's situation in this country, was that she was frustrated. It left her in a position to either do something desperate or just entirely give in and let the system do what it will do.

So if you were to say " Who killed Rosebud" we'd have to start pretty far back and go dip into the whole society, not just the trigger-happy guy that they sent in knowing he was scared to begin with ?

Yes. You know who killed Rosebud? The same people who killed Lincoln, to Kennedy, Malcolm X, Martin Luther King, Fred Hampton. Different bodies, different conspiracy, different plans, but basically the same, you know—those people that feed on hate. People so fearful of the underdog that they'd do anything, anything—and they got the power to do anything to suppress it. Rosebud was indeed a victim, we're all victims, you know.

Do you remember the last time that you saw her?

Well, that was the time that we went to Willard Park and we had a long discussion and she really didn't want to hear nothing about God. But I'm a very Godly individual and I kinda insisted. We talked for a long time, she could've just got up and ran away, you know? And I knew something was troubling her, I knew that something was on her mind. And I indirectly could visualize it. I couldn't map it out completely but I knew there was something she wanted to do, something that she felt that she had to do, you know, for the people. I didn't know she'd try to do it alone. And that was a detrimental part, see. She had to weigh it and kept within the community of the people and organized and got the people motivated. We could've all done it together.

What do you think made her act alone that day?

I think that she was so disenchanted, I mean—she was so disillusioned with the movement at the time. Most people were very rhetorical, as opposed to going out there doing direct action, see. Now there was only very few of us that was doing the direct action, you know, trying to raise the consciousness of the people, see? But most people, you know, they just came out for the meetings and—people we knew, you know, people that we admired as revolutionaries. But we saw them in a rhetorical light, as opposed to being out there physically, being amongst the people, and doin' for the people—being a servant of the people. Like, " I, Rosebud", Andy, and David Nadel, and Carol, and that brother right there, Ray, and, you know, Eli and people like that, who are actually out there physically in the battle, you know. So I think that kind of messed her around, you know. But she had a strong love for us. I was gone at the time, like I said, so she couldn't come to me and confide in me of her directness in that action. But she had before, you know, came to me and talked to me about something that she was planning, and one time, you know, she told me something like that, and I listened to it, and I told her it wasn't well-thought-out, it had to be planned.

I'm told that she was a good writer. Have you ever read anything she wrote?

Yes, indeed. I have one piece of her writing, a flyer. She helped me organize the Berkeley Homeless Union.

What was the happiest moment that you ever remember with her?

Oh, there's a lot of moments. I think her happiest moment was when she came to my political table and she'd probably be kinda upset about the day, and I'd kinda pick up on it, you know. And I'd say, "Rosebud, let's go down here to Fred's and get some chocolate, I'll buy you some chocolate." And then she'd say, "Oh, wow! You know I never turn down chocolate," and her whole face would light up. But, yeah, like I said, in those last days, she was becoming more and more questioning of every situation. She was becoming distant from a lot of her friends, even me. She thought I wanted to get in her pants, as opposed to being her friend, see. And I don't know what provoked that fear, because I've never even had that thought on my mind, you know. I wanted to be her friend because I really enjoyed her spirit. She was a warrior, you know, and I really appreciated that. There's still warriors out here, you know, but the African

Americanas out here, a lot of them are not interested in the revolution like they were in the 60's when I was involved with the Panthers and stuff. A lot of them are just into the alcohol or what I call the genocidal drug, crack. I can't relate to them, you know, so I normally hang with other people like me, people like Rosebud, Andy, Bob, David and the progressive people like that.

What do you think makes some people strong enough to try to fight the system and others be enveloped by it?

Well for one, I think that some people are provoked into actions, you know, just by their circumstances alone. And a lot of people, like me, were just born into it. See, I come from a long line of warriors. One of my great, great, great, great, great, great ancestors was Hannibal Barker, and he went against the Romans. And my people that was kidnapped from Africa when they came over here, they escaped the slave owners. They went on Indian land and mingled with the Indians.

What made Rosebud become a revolutionary?

She was different. Her parents saw the difference in her, you know, when she was seven years old. She was beginning to formulate her own thoughts, her own identity and stuff. It wasn't necessarily very clear, 'cause even in her last days, her perspective wasn't as clear as it should've been, I don't know if that's the correct way to say it. She was depressed and she was being hounded by the police. One day the cops heard her mention to other people about where she was crashing. So they deliberately went up there to find her, and they found her and made her move on, and they harassed her that whole night. So she was tired. Physically exhausted, you know.

They didn't try to help her at all?
They hated Rosebud. They hated her because of her ideas, just like they hate me for my ideas.

The Free Speech stage in the park, this platform, which symbolizes the origin of the Free Speech movement in America, is a place where people are actually still being killed by inches even before the bullet hits.
That's right. They're being killed psychologically by unconcerned governments who have absolutely no interest in alleviating suffering.

This is a powerful question, but what was your saddest moment with her before that happened?
Well, my saddest moment is where—at Willard Park. I sensed doom in the air; I sensed something terrible and I begged her to come away with me. I was going on a spiritual retreat... but then she started accusing me of wanting to, uh, be next to her sexually. I was really frustrated at this point, you know... and I said, " Well, believe there's no God. How do you suppose you got here?" And she said, " My mother fucked my father." I said, " Well, how do you think they got here?" And, you know, she went on and said the same thing. All the way back. So on, so on, so on. So I said, " Well, don't you think there was a Supreme Being that put all that in existence?" She said "No." That was my saddest time with her. She didn't quite understand where I was coming from and she

couldn't—didn't understand what God had given her. It was frustrating and very painful. But now she's in the Spirit well, she's not among us anymore. You know, she was one of my strongest soldiers. I was there with her from the beginning, you know. We helped kick off some stuff in the park, and really opened people's minds about the situation here in Berkeley. Our trip was to try to do something for the people, keep up some type of movement. And we done that, you know. But like I said, people frustrated her. That's why I'm not as politically active as I was in the past, you know—though I want to go back into the battle, and with real soldiers, you know.

Chapter Twelve
Autopsy Part II

The fingernails are extremely closely clipped, intact, and with only black material observable beneath them. No binding indentation sites are present about the arms or hands. No smoke, powder, or stippling is identified on either arm or hand. No needle puncture marks are present. No hyperpigmented scars are present over accessible veins. No further blunt injuries are noted to arms or hands. Law enforcement personnel (prior to examination of the hands) performed chemical tests for trace material. This to a certain extent involved disruption of the previously described areas of blood and black material. Clipping of the fingernails is performed after this.

The back is without further abnormalities.

INTERNAL EXAMINATION

The body is opened through the usual Y-shaped incision. Except for gunshot wounds no abnormalities are noted.

GUNSHOT WOUND SUMMARY

WOUND #1
TYPE: Entrance gunshot wound.

LOCATION: Midline of the back.

DIRECTION: From the back of the body to the front of the body, from the left side of the body to the right side of the body at a 5° angle, and from the feet upward towards the top of the head at a 10° angle.

AREAS INVOLVED: Thoracic vertebral column, spinal cord, right pleural cavity, right lung, right rib one.

EXIT: this gunshot wound exits at exit wound #6.

BULLET: Most of the bullet exits the body. Small metallic fragments are recovered in the parenchyma of the right lung. These are retained for evidence in a sealed envelope.

This is a hemorrhagic gunshot wound.

No smoke or powder is noted along the path of the entrance wound.

DESCRIPTION: This gunshot wound enters in the midline of the back. The bullet passes through the thoracic vertebral column, causing a partial severance to the spinal cord. It passes into the posterior medial aspect of the right pleural cavity in the area of %-3. Bone fragments are pushed in the direction of the bullet. It passes through the right upper lobe of the lung. Metallic fragments are noted in the posterior aspect of the lung. The bullet path through the lung is about 1 inch in diameter. It involves moderate-sized airways and vessels. It exits the anterior surface of the lung. From here it exits the right pleural cavity by passing through right rib one. The bone fragments from the rib are pushed in the direction of the bullet. The bullet then continues and exits the body at wound #6. Other than the small metallic fragments previously described in the lung, no bullet is recovered.

OTHER: In association with this gunshot wound there is a 300 cc right hemothorax.

WOUND #2

TYPE: Entrance gunshot wound.

LOCATION: Posterior aspect of the right shoulder.

DIRECTION: From the back of the body towards the front of the body, from the head downward towards the feet at a 40° angle, and from the right side of the body towards the left side of the body at a 45° angle.

Areas involved: Musculature and connective tissue of the right shoulder, musculature and connective tissue of the torso, right humerus, right pleural cavity, pericardial sac, heart, left pleural cavity, and left rib four.

EXIT: None.

BULLET: A deformed, large, brass colored and gray bullet is recovered in the left front side of the chest. it is retained for evidence in a sealed envelope.

This is a hemorrhagic gunshot wound.

No smoke or powder is noted along the path of the entrance wound.

DESCRIPTION: This gunshot wound enters the back side of the right shoulder. The bullet passes through the musculature and connective tissue in this area of the body. It causes a grazing-type defect to the superior head of the right humerus. It enters the right pleural cavity, passing through the intercostal space of right ribs four and five. The ribs are not fractured. It passes through the right upper lobe of the lung in its inferior aspect. It passes just beneath the pleural surface on the anterior side. It then passes into the lateral aspect of the right side of the pericardial sac through a 1 inch defect. It enters at the lateral aspect of the right atrium. It causes a grazing defect to the anterior wall of the right atrium that penetrates into the atrial chamber. it then continues and causes a contusion to the anterior surface of the right ventricle but without grazing the surface of the right ventricle. This is just below the base of the aorta. From here it exits the periocardic sac through its left lateral side through a 1 inch defect. It enters the left pleural cavity. It does not cause a defect to the lung. It then immediately exits the left pleural cavity through the intercostal space between left ribs three and four, causing a fracture defect to left rib four. The lateral segment of this fracture is pushed outwardly in the direction of the bullet. It is in this area that the bullet is recovered.

OTHER: In order for this gunshot track to be possible, the right shoulder must be brought forward several inches from its normal anatomical position. In association with this gunshot wound is a 100 cc hemopericardium, a 400 cc left hemothorax and a 300 cc right hemothorax.

WOUND #4
TYPE: Entrance gunshot wound.
LOCATION: Right side of the neck.
DIRECTION: From the right side of the body towards the left side of the body, from the head downward towards the feet at a 45° angle, and from the front of the body towards the back of the body at a 45° angle.
Areas involved: Musculature and connective tissue of neck and torso, trachea.
EXIT: None.

BULLET: a large, deformed, brass and gray colored bullet is recovered in the soft tissue of the left side of the chest. It is retained for evidence in a sealed envelope.

This is a hemorrhagic gunshot wound.

No smoke or powder is noted along the path of the entrance wound.

DESCRIPTION: This gunshot wound enters in the right front side of the neck. The bullet causes a grazing defect to the trachea. There is an open area here measuring 1 inch in greatest dimension. It continues through the neck anterior to the carotid bundle. From here it passes posterior to the left clavicle. It does not penetrate into body cavities.

Chapter Thirteen
Teddy Remembers

 was still in jail the day Rosebud died. The first thing the guards did was take her letters. I didn't know what was going on. They took her letters that same morning and four hours later they came and got me and, and brought me down to the captain. He's this big, fat obnoxious pig and he's laughing and gloating while he's telling me that the girl I write to was shot and killed by the police. And I just went berserk. I picked up a chair and hit him with it. I had to do another year because of that. But I'd have done it in the hole if I had to. They gave back the letters I guess they just made copies and sent them off somewhere. I don't know where.

We met at 2626 Regent Street. I was in the penitentiary for four months for parole violation. When I was getting out my friend Johnny wrote me a letter saying that he had rented a couple of rooms at 2626 Regent Street and that when I got out I could move in. I got out in December of '90 and moved into that house. Rosebud had moved in two weeks before. She'd just come to Berkeley from Lexington, Kentucky via Portland. She'd stopped in Portland, Oregon for a while. We became friends and got closer and closer. About three months later we became lovers. We remained lovers until her death.

But you were in jail the last few months of her life. I can't believe I knew nothing about this because I must have interviewed maybe forty people and nobody mentioned you. Of the group down at Long Haul did anybody know you? Elisa or Steve? You don't know any of those people?

No.

Everybody's said she worked incessantly for the things she believed in and kept her personal life pretty much out of it. What do you think made her so depressed at that time?

Being on the street. Lack of, oh, support from people. Lack of commitment from people. I don't believe that it was suicide. No way.

When was the last letter she wrote you?

August 6.

So it was the same month – She died on August 25. Some of the other letters say that she loves you.

This was her last note:

"Teddy, Aaaah! Miss you. Things for me are still the same. Nothing's happened with the park as yet. Nothing's happened on the anniversary of the volleyball courts going in. Trying to keep busy. Got several projects going. A friend of mine is teaching me calculus. Sorry for not writing so much as I should. Haven't had much to write about. Had a cold but I think it's gone. I love you. That's about it. Bye, Rosebud."

It doesn't sound like she was that depressed, does it?

No, it sounds like she's making plans and continuing them.

Uh, huh. Well that knocks the previous theory out, it really does. I guess if it were legal it would be called something like "introduction of new evidence".

She was my friend, my lover, my partner, my mother, my daughter, my teacher, my student. She was all those things.

Let's get back to... you met her when you were both staying at the same house. Now wasn't there a bust there for so-called explosives or something? Her attorney told me it was hardly more than firecrackers.

I think she had a gas can with some gas in it and that's why she got kicked out of Regent Street. That was in June of '91. I was in prison in Susanville at the time.

What was the charge?

Rosebud wanted us to get a car. She had some political action she wanted to do with a car and I went and broke into a jewelry store trying to get the money together. I got caught.

How long was the sentence?

It wasn't too bad. From April to November.

You know, I have a little bit of footage of Rosebud herself, uh, but, the there is only a bit of sound that I have of her because some idiot was saying "soundcheck, soundcheck" over everything that she was saying. I salvaged one sentence. She's saying, "Berkeley's the only place in the world where if you're a socialist you're more to the right than to the left."

That sounds like Rosebud.

Yes, she had a sense of humor. So you were still in San Quentin at the time she died. When did you go in?

I got out in November of '91 and I went back in May of '92, well, actually, April of '92. I went back to Santa Rita and then I went back to San Quentin, right before her death. August of '92.

So did the indictment mean anything political or was it just for the armed robberies?

The motive was political. In S.D.S. we always left the icon flags behind us when we did the armed robberies so they'd knew it was political. The way we looked at it in my old collectives is that a revolutionary survived through his attack, and cut oneself off. We didn't accept liberal support, or money from the ACLU or whatever. One survived alone through one's attack if one was a revolutionary. That was our collective philosophy. In S.D.S. and later we did armed robberies, and computer frauds. One time we set up a company and registered it with the city. We rented a check writing machine and got a telephone answering service and a mailing address. We got a company I.D. So with the company I.D. we opened up savings accounts, and then, then with the savings accounts and the company I.D., we opened up individual checking accounts at a commercial bank. We had a thousand dollars in a business account in another commercial bank so they gave us a book of checks, right? The first week everybody got a check for two hundred and twenty dollars, and went around cashing them. We got the money back together and put it back in the account. The second week same thing. We each got one check for two-hundred and twenty dollars, cashed them and put them back in the account. The third week we each got twenty-five checks and got the telephone book and looked at every branch of First National Bank on the island of Manhattan, which had, like, a hundred and one branches, right? We got our maps together and our routes and between nine and twelve, we turned that one thousand in the account into thirty-six thousand by cashing payroll checks in the line between nine and twelve. Knowing them, their first computer check would be at twelve o' clock. Of course at twelve o' clock they knew something was wrong.

Who thought that one out?
Just a guy named Joe. As a matter of fact our collective had no leaders but for ideas he was a leader. He was a very intelligent creative revolutionary and first got involved in politics during the Mississippi Civil Rights demonstrations in 1964 when he went to help get people registered to vote.

Wasn't that the summer that Shwerner and Goodman were killed?
This was all from 1968 to 1970.

Okay, so let's get a further chronology.
I came to Berkeley in 1970. I wasn't into robbing banks or blowing up buildings like my collective was in New York. The first thing I did was street theatre. The piece was called "Burning City Theatre." We did the play in laundrymats and supermarkets and on the street.

Do you have any kids?

I have one son who is twenty six years, old and he's in New York. His mother and I were never really a couple, we were in the collective and when she left the collective she married a college professor who adopted my son, so haven't seen him in years.

What happened from 1978 until you met Rosebud?

I remember tearing up the asphalt in People's Park in 1979. When the parking lot was where the garden is now. I got here six months too late for Bloody Thursday, but in May of '72 they put up another fence that was a twelve-foot high cyclone fence. Michael and I were together, standing next to each other as we tore it down. A lot of people joined us.

So you have a long history of park actions, too? What was your life like from the time you got here until you met Rosebud?

I lived with one woman from 1971 'til 1978. She and I were very together in our revolutionary fervor until the time she became a lawyer. Then she got a little more cautious.

You've always written poetry, Teddy?

Since I was about sixteen. I used to publish in the school literary magazine and was the editor in my senior year. And Berrigan helped me a lot with it. He's a great poet.

What was happening in Rosebud's life until the time that

you landed back in prison?
She was so happy to be here at first. She'd finally made it to California, to Berkeley, where she thought she could do some good.

What do you think happened?
She and I argued about this particular action for a year and a half.

She had mentioned it before?
Many times.

Well, you know, only to you. Nobody else spoke of it. She had never mentioned it to anybody else.
Well we argued about going in there and trashing the place because as retaliation for the trashing of the park. She was convinced she had checked it out and looked at all the windows, and she was sure the place didn't have an alarm. I would say to her, "Rosebud, it has to have an alarm system. This is the University of California. These people have the technology and the money to totally protect themselves." But she would never quite believe it. She was stubborn, you know, she had a stubborn streak.

Do you think she intended to hurt the chancellor?
No, she was just gonna trash the place. Like a symbolic gesture.

Every image that I have of her is smiling.
She had a thousand-watt smile.

So you don't buy the theory that she was suicidal the day she broke into the chancellor's mansion?

Not at all. What a lie that is. That's the lie of those who murdered her.

What happened then didn't have to happen at all. It would've been simply a misdemeanor. Or would they have turned it into a felony?

The worst thing they could've charged her with is home invasion which is a felony. Given her youth and lack of serious record, she would've done a couple of years, maybe.

So you don't disapprove of her going in? Well, what about that machete?

I argued with her about not doing it. I don't know anything about the machete. It's a good thing for trashing a house. Like for tearing up furniture, and slashing stuff on the walls.

You feel that that's all she intended to do?
Yes.

Did she ever talk about, you know, killing or hurting somebody?

She never wanted to kill anyone. She felt that in a revolution there might be times that you might have to hurt someone in self-defense.

But that would be very different than going in with a machete intending to kill the chancellor

That's not her at all.

So that was heartbreaking. She was so young.
Three years later I'm just beginning to heal.

I'm still confused because of all the people I interviewed, nobody said anything about you being her boyfriend. Though I hadn't interviewed any of the people who lived on Regent Street.
They wouldn't have told you about me. Her lawyer not only knew of our involvement but he helped me get money to her while I was in jail. I'd sent her five hundred dollars right before she died. It was money that I made while I was out and I had it on me when they arrested me. I wanted to get it to her since I didn't need it in jail. Everybody in jail said, "Hey, what're you, crazy? Everybody else here is getting their money sent in; you're getting your money sent out." I said, "She needs it more than I do." What I did was go to my counselor and say "I owe my lawyer money." Her lawyer verified it and I sent two checks to him.

Chapter Fourteen

Everyone Remembers IV

nce she was out of jail Rosebud had moved to the Info Cafe, a radical commune in North Oakland. She stayed active in the People's Park movement and she and Andy pitched a tent in People's Park Annex, a vacant lot formerly occupied by a burned out hotel. It had been taken over by homeless people a few weeks before.

The cops were always watching Rosebud. A month after she got out of Santa Rita she was re-arrested for resisting a cop. Her friends again bailed her out.

She helped begin to build the People's Bathroom in the Park but cops ripped it up as soon as construction was begun.

When the Annex was dismantled by cops in the Spring of '92, Rosebud and Andy moved to People's Park. They spent their days in the grove west of the driveway entrance. There were lots of homeless people who spent time there.

University cops kept a close watch on the Grove. They stopped there every day making arrests on small pretexts.

During what was to be the last few days of her life, Rosebud was almost constantly harassed by the police.

Dream or nightmare? I won't ever sleep. I was lying there worrying about my coming court case when they shone their flashlight in my eyes. "Get moving Denovo"they said. It wasn't a great night for finding a new place to sleep. Not many stars.

Chapter Fifteen
Don't Cry Andy

hy did they send in a cop who was already paranoid because he'd been shot five times by a burglary suspect? Why did they send in a cop who already had a history of complaints against him. Including (as William had said before) a complaint actually sustained by the Police Review commission and the City Manager, of his excessive force.

The cops hated and feared little Rosebud. Tiny as she was, she could and did get in their face whenever she felt they were doing wrong

All her friends had pointed out that calling officers from Oakland to finish the job, seemed like the UC cops didn't want to be personally responsible to the community.

Usual procedure since the house had been emptied, would have been to encircle it, send in tear gas, call her family or friends to negotiate, and call in a mediation team.

Rosebud, small fierce organizer of street people, diligent worker towards a society less Grapes of Wrath-like than she'd found in her introduction to California, how

could her young life been saved?
Rosebud, how could we have saved you?
I pledge convenience
to the gag of the United States of America
and to the Dissension for which it stands
one devastation, under Sod, incorrigible,
with slavedom and injustice last call.

Don't cry Andy, don't cry.
We slept in a tent at People's Park Annex before they closed it
down, remember?. But at the end we were sleeping in the hills.
We weren't bothering anyone. Except, of course, in the daytime
we were fighting for the Park.

The violence that erupted after they shot Rosebud, was
like no violence that had ever erupted in Berkeley before.
It was different from Bloody Thursday, in the 60s.

Goosey goosey gander
wither shall Rosebud wander
upstairs and downstairs
and in the Chancellor's chamber
There she met a scared cop
who wouldn't say his prayers
who shot her in the chest and back
to quiet down his fears.

THE COPS WATCHED ME ALL THE TIME.
I DON'T LIKE BEING WATCHED
I KNOW THEY'RE OUT TO GET ME,

I'M NOT IMAGINING IT. THEY ACT LIKE THEY'RE OUT TO GET ME.
MY COURT DATE COMING UP SOON.

There was not a word or a hint from her, she just seemed quiet and like she was going to want some space for the rest of the night.
Where'd she go?
Where do people go when they die?
This is going to turn out to be a suspense story after all
Where is the suspense? Rosebud's already been killed and we know it.
Okay, dig, the suspense is this. See she didn't believe in heaven or hell but does her not believing in it make it unhappen, or is she already in heaven because it's the place for lost beautiful souls whether she believed it or no?

I'M SURE SHE'S IN HEAVEN ANDY, DON'T CRY.

I CRY EVEN WHEN MY EYES DON'T, BECAUSE SHE WAS TOO YOUNG TO DIE,

THAT'S RIGHT ANDY, WHEN PEOPLE DIE YOUNG IT NEVER SEEMS NATURAL THOUGH IN NATURE IT HAPPENS ALL THE TIME.

DON'T CRY CLAIRE, FILMMAKERS AREN'T SUPPOSED TO CRY, ONLY THE ONES WHO SEE THEIR FILMS ARE SUPPOSED TO,

I'M NOT CRYING ANDY THAT'S JUST MY OWN PAST CAUSING AN UPHEAVAL ON MY FACE

YA CAN'T FOOL ME YA KNOW, CLAIRE, YOU

THINK ROSEBUD'S YOUR CHILD.

OK ANDY, ROSEBUD'S ALL MY DAUGHTERS
AND THE WARRIOR OF MY SOUL.

Chapter Sixteen

Autopsy Part Three

WOUND #5

TYPE: Entrance gunshot wound.

LOCATION: Right front side of the chest.

DIRECTION: From the front of the body towards the back of the body, from the left side of the body towards the right side of the body at a 45° angle, and from the head downward towards the feet at a 20° angle.

AREAS INVOLVED: Musculature and connective tissue of torso.

EXIT: This gunshot wound exits at exit wound #3 in the right axillary area.

BULLET: None recovered.

This is a hemorrhagic gunshot wound.

No smoke or powder is noted along the path of the entrance wound.

DESCRIPTION: This gunshot wound enters in the right front side of the chest. The bullet passes through toe subcutaneous tissue and musculature of the torso. It passes inferior to the axillary bundle. It also passes medial to the humerus. It exits at exit wound #3.

WOUND #7

TYPE: Grazing gunshot wound.

LOCATION: Lateral aspect of the left index finger.

DIRECTION: Not determined.

AREAS INVOLVED: Connective tissue, tendon, and bone of left index finger.

BULLET: None recovered.

This is a hemorrhagic gunshot wound.

No smoke or powder is noted along the path of the entrance wound.

DESCRIPTION: This gunshot wound causes extensive disruption of the right fifth finger. The tip of the finger is traumatically absent as a result of the gunshot wound. Most of the middle and distal phalanges are likewise absent. There is comminuated fracturing of the proximal phalanx. This gunshot wound has caused absence of much of the finger in its lateral one-half.

BODY CAVITIES: The pleural cavities, pericardial cavity, and peritoneal cavity are lined by smooth, glistening surfaces. The remaining ribs are nonremarkable. The diaphragms are intact.

HEART: In situ, the heart is normal. The apex is at the left midclavicular line. The heart weighs 300 grams. The epicardial surface is smooth and glistening. Ventricular myocardium is brown. Chambers are normal. Valves are normal. No left ventricular hypertrophy is present. No asymmetric hypertrophy is present. No myxoid degeneration of the mitral valve is present. No vegetations are present on valve leaflets. Coronary ostia are patent. The coronary system has its usual anatomical distribution and is nonremarkable. No thrombi are present. Except for the gunshot wound no abnormalities are identified.

VESSELS: The aorta and tributaries are nonremarkable. The pulmonary artery and venous system contain no thromboemboli.

TRACHEA AND BRONCHI: No further abnormalities. Lined by pale yellow mucosal surfaces.

LUNGS: The lungs are of normal size. Pleural surfaces are smooth. Lung parenchyma is congested and edematous. Lung parenchyma contains no areas of consolidation. No pulmonary infarcts are present. No bronchial asthma is identified. Airways of both lungs are nonremarkable and no tumors are present. The arterial system of both lungs is opened and no thromboemboli or other abnormalities are identified. Except for the gunshot wounds no abnormalities are identified. Except for the gunshot wounds, no abnormalities are noted.

ORAL CAVITY: The teeth are natural. None are acutely missing or loose. No abnormalities of the oral cavity are identified. Palpitation of the maxilla and the mandible reveals no abnormalities.

ESOPHAGUS: Lined by a white, wrinkled mucosal surface.

STOMACH: Contains 100 cc of pasty red-brown food material, admixed with small amounts of hemorrhage. The mucosal surface is tan. No tumors are noted. No ulcers are present.

INTESTINES: Covered by smooth serosal surfaces. The intestines are opened, and no abnormalities are noted.

LIVER: Weighs 1100 grams. The serosal surface is smooth and glistening. The parenchyma is brown and pale, consistent with ischemia. The anterior margin is sharp. No tumors are present. No fatty metamorphosis is present. No cirrhosis is present.

GALLBLADDER: The gallbladder is of normal size. Its surface is smooth. Its wall is of normal thickness. It is lined by a green velvety mucosal surface. It contains 5 cc of thick green bile. No stones are present.

PANCREAS: The pancreas is of normal size. Its parenchyma is yellow-brown and lobulated. No tumors are present. No saponification is noted.

SPLEEN: The spleen is of normal size. Its capsule is gray and wrinkled. Its parenchyma is red-purple and soft.

ADRENAL GLANDS: Normal in size and triangular in shape. Sectioning reveals nonremarkable cortex and medullary parts. No hemorrhages are present.

KIDNEYS: The kidneys are of normal size. Surfaces are smooth. Parenchyma is brown and pale, consistent with ischemia. There is a distinct corticomedullary separation. Papillae are normal The calyces and pelves of both kidneys are nonremarkable. No obvious abnormalities are noted of the ureters. No stones are present.

BLADDER: The bladder contains a scant amount of urine. It is lined by a tan mucosal surface. No trabeculation or tumors are present. No diverticula are noted.

FEMALE REPRODUCTIVE ORGANS: The reproductive organs are removed en bloc, along with the rectum. The vagina is lined by a white, wrinkled mucosal surface with no abnormalities. The uterus is of normal size. Sectioning of it reveals no abnormalities. No products of conception are noted. The ovaries are of normal size and no corpora lutea of pregnancy are identified.

MUSCULOSKELETAL SYSTEM: The pleural surfaces are stripped. Individual ribs are dissected around, and no further abnormalities are identified. The rectus abdominis muscle is cross-sectioned and no abnormalities are noted.

NECK: The soft tissue about the larynx is nonremarkable except for the hemorrhage from gunshot wound #4. The individual laryngeal structures are intact and nonremarkable. The larynx is lined by a pale yellow mucosal surface. No foreign material is present in the larynx. The cervical vertebral column is normal. The thyroid gland is of normal size. Sectioning of it reveals a nonremarkable red-brown parenchyma.

CENTRAL NERVOUS SYSTEM: Soft tissue about the cranial vault is normal. The brain weighs 1300 grams. The gyri and sulci of the cerebral hemispheres are normal. Sectioning of the brain reveals no abnormalities. No contusions are noted. The ventricular system of the brain is nonremarkable. No subdural or subarachnoid hemorrhages are present. The vessels at the base of the brain are nonremarkable. Stripping the dural from the inner table of the skull reveals no abnormalities.

SPECIMENS TAKEN:
1)   Blood from hemothorax
2)   Leg: blood
3)   Stomach content
4)   Liver
5   Bile
6)   Urine
7)   Tissue
8)   Histology sections
9)   Photos

EVIDENCE COLLECTED:
1)   Hair from eyebrows and eyelashes
2)   Scalp hair
3)   Blood
4)   Black material from body
5)   Metal from right side of face
6)   Pubic brush and pubic combings
7)   Metallic fragments from right lung
8)   Nail clippings
9)   Smears and swabs of oral, vaginal, and rectal cavities
10)   Two bullets
        1)   Anterior chest
        2)   Left chest

Thomas Wayne Rogers, M.D.

Chapter Seventeen
Carol Remembers

The sad thing about Rosebud was that had she lived, she might have changed her approach. I don't know if 'change' is the right word. I say this because I'm almost forty. She was young enough that I don't think it was easy for her to imagine how you could be an extremely rebellious and independent person, and somehow find a way to survive. And I think that she eventually would have found a way. I think she was that resourceful.

What was remarkable about her is that she was not your classic heroine. And I don't think you could really describe her fairly without including little things like the fact that she had a stutter. She never seemed particularly embarrassed by it, but it was a part of how she spoke. It may be part of the reason she wasn't a public speaker like a lot of the people she hung out with. But it was, (along with the thick Kentucky accent) a part of who she was.

I don't think you could demonstrate very well how she became such a symbol, when before her death she really was, you know, one of the people who worked behind the scenes and shoveled the coal, and did the hard work without really looking for glory or fame out of it.

I don't think it crossed her mind to be well-known in terms of being an activist, though she was often the one

who led the charge. She just wanted to work for the causes in which she believed. She wanted to be a part of a
community, and gave it everything she had. I think that's
one thing that was outstanding about her.

And I think she did find a community of people who
were doing that, who had pretty much sacrificed everything to create a community of dissent, and to work hard
towards illuminating an alternative point of view.

I must have met her before the new U. C. Park construction began on July 31st, 1991. I have a vague memory of her being a part of these enormous and excruciating
meetings in People's Park. I don't recall her making big
speeches at those meetings. I don't recall her even saying
a whole lot. Nor did *I* say a whole lot, except to go on
about non-violence and warn people endlessly in that
way. But I remember her being there at almost any
demonstration, and being willing to do whatever it took
to support a demonstrations.

*Could you describe the night they first took down the Free
Box and what happened after that?*
The first I heard about this new battle at People's Park
was when I saw a picture of the chancellor and mayor
shaking hands. All I could think to myself was "What?
Uh-oh!"

And the first I knew that it had actually created a
change up at People's Park was when they tore out the
Free Box. And I got a call from Andrea of Copwatch,
and she said, "You've got to come up. They're destroying
the Free Box (free clothing in the park for the homeless)
every night, and we're rebuilding it everyday. This really

matters, and you've got to come up. But I was too ill to come up so I was getting reports. Different people were calling me and saying, "It's really happening. You've got to be up there now." That's what drew me up to the Park for these meetings that began to happen at 5 o'clock. People tried to prepare for the final destruction of the park. In my opinion what the University calls "development " of the Park is destruction. That's when I began to slowly get to know there were people who cared, who would come out. And it was a very diverse group of people. We didn't know each other's names and we didn't need to.

In the Park you told me about asking Rosebud to state the First Amendment.

Do you mean where she talked about the Amendments? Well, we were down at Blake Street where Community Defense, Incorporated, had its offices. Rosebud was working as a volunteer for us. We were sitting on the porch having a smoke break, and I remember saying to somebody, "I've gotta get a copy of the Bill of Rights because I'm getting all my Amendments mixed up. I can't remember which is which."

And Rosebud laughed and said, "I know them all. I have them down." She said, "The first Amendment is the one they break when they throw you in jail for posting a flyer. The second one is the one they break when they throw you in jail for carrying a pocket knife. The third is the one they break..." And she went on and on and on. It's my memory that she went through them all though she would abbreviate some of them by saying, "And this

Amendment is just like that Amendment." But you could tell she'd been through this before. This was second nature to her. And I was very impressed. The whole crowd on the porch just listened to her rattle 'em off. She knew her stuff.

Everybody that I've spoken to – everybody, except the people at UC, said that she was not only not mentally disturbed, but she was extraordinarily intelligent.

She was a gifted student. She did attend college – a year or two of college. I can completely relate to attending a year or two of college and then deciding to move on. That's what I did too.

There's a point at which the books just don't cut it, and you have to get your hands into something, to really see something accomplished. There was an extreme impatience on her part to see something done and to awaken the community. And that's where we really failed. This community rolled over and went to sleep during a grotesque crackdown on the poorest and most vulnerable part of Berkeley's population, and just allowed it to happen . And that's where I think Rosebud stood out, in that she was not only an advocate for the rights of people without shelter and without funds, but she decided to stay with them, and just be there and be a part of it, because she knew that what was happening was wrong.

We moved here in '79. We were told to come to Berkeley because we would be accepted here. But Berkeley changed before my very eyes, and became more like the places we were leaving.

It's happening everywhere, I think.

Not totally—yet. Because there are still people like you and Rosebud.
But we've been successfully marginalized so that...

What do you mean by marginalized?
Oh, people see views like mine as "radical." People like Rosebud are marginalized in the press and turned into monsters. That this most idealistic of young women was portrayed as a monster, prevented a real investigation surrounding her death, which might have made it clear that her death was completely unnecessary.

Andy said he saw her the night before, that they had made up a quarrel they'd had, and were friends that night, so they were treating each other gently... and that she said she needed to be by herself for a while, but there was not a glimmer of her intent. He had no idea what was going to happen. He was also very bitter that her friends did not have any way of getting there and persuading her to come out. They were never asked to negotiate or send friends to help her. You see it in all the Hollywood movies, for God's sake. They send friends and family.with loudspeakers, or bull horns, saying, "Come out." And if she was so-called "disturbed," she needed to be taken to the hospital and then within a couple of days,be given a hearing. He also said that she was very very frightened because she had that possible two-year jail sentence hanging over her. And he put his head back and he said, "She was not a person who could be locked up. She needed to be free.
She was so scared about prison, and had even talked about

it that night.

It would make sense in terms of the timing that the trial was weighing on her – the upcoming trial.

He said it was weighing on her terribly, and that she couldn't face being locked up for any amount of time. Maybe because she had been locked in a psych ward when she was twelve on the advice of a shrink

That's what I've been thinking. She'd been there, and she'd had a terrible time with institutions. It seemed as though it was a game that she knew how to play if she had to, but it was a horrible, cruel, and humiliating game. Prison is the same way.

I had the same experience Andy had, seeing her just two days before August 25th, having a normal conversation with her and making an arrangement to exchange some notes. Notes from some meeting. Having no idea, hearing nothing about any plan, hearing nothing about any special amount of pressure.

I was really impressed by the statement you made, in the park. You said if had been three fraternity boys, they certainly would have negotiated.

Hell, yeah.

But as soon as they knew that it was Rosebud, there was no chance?

Yes. As soon as they knew it was Rosebud, the plan changed. Her life didn't matter to them. Fraternity boys would have mattered. Frat pranks would've been handled differently, but Rosebud… you know.

So, as soon as they knew who she was they sent in this trig-ger-happy cop?

That's the way it looks to me. After talking to every-body, that's sure the way it looks to me. The U.C. people have their explanation, of course.

Well I talked to the head of the U.C. Police – the woman. She said all the predictable, usual things. "You know we were very lucky that were able to save the chancellor and his wife. But they were already out of the house.

You know, in order to promote that myth, you really have to not have seen Rosebud. I don't care if she had a machine gun. She was so tiny, and you could have disarmed her, you know, with a stick. And I don't believe…I don't care what they say, I don't believe she was in there to kill anybody. I think she was making a gesture, showing them how it felt for her space to be invaded. I don't believe that she had in the back of her mind as her goal to kill *anybody*. But I do think that she wanted something to happen in the hardest way. And she was tired of complacency.

Here it was a solid year, and what was happening? Nothing! I remember a feeling of doldrums around the park and a feeling of great loss—even though we had won the open space, and we had saved the Free Speech stage. People forget that. But without the protest that we managed to pull together, there would be no more open space; there would be no more stage.

But it was hard to celebrate those victories when you had these automatons actually being *paid* to play volley-

ball. And that's what was happening. It was harder to put
on free concerts because of the SLAPP suit. And David
Nadel had been such a stalwart mover behind so many of
the concerts. His time, money, and energy that had
helped to put them on so regularly the year before, as a
way to make the Park bloom. Concerts were a way to
make people understand what the Park was really about.
People coming together to share music and speeches.

There was less of that happening, thanks to the SLAPP
suit. It was driving all of us nuts. We were all doing our
best to cope. We were scattered all over the city at different committee meetings, trying to figure out where we
could do a little good. And it was hard. It was even hard to
figure out what we had accomplished. And hard to feel
anything but defeated. That was a special pressure on her,
because she was so impatient and so young.

I think you should tell something about the SLAPP suit.
Well, the way I see it, I'm one of four people being
sued by the University of California in Berkeley. It's me,
David Nadel, who runs the music club Ashkenaz, Mike
Lee, who's a desktop publisher, and Bob Sparks, who's
been a community activist for all his life practically, and
works as a maintenance engineer.

We didn't know each other before the new U. C. yup-
pie construction began at People's Park, but they decided
that we four formed the conspiracy that created the
opposition to development in People's Park. It makes it
sound like we sat down in a little room and planned all of
the four days of general civil unrest that followed the July
31st, 1991 riots, when in fact, three of us just went to jail

peacefully with the first 36 people arrested. I don't know where Mike Lee was, but we didn't even know each other. We just all sort of walked onto the bus and spent the next days in jail.

Well, meantime, Berkeley's on fire, and I guess they're attributing all of that energy and all of that resistance to us. And all I can say is, it's ludicrous. People never did take orders from me, and they sure don't now.

All that happened, in *my* opinion, is that the University of California decided that since throwing us in jail didn't stop us, and beating us up didn't stop us, and rubber bullets didn't stop us, they had to try a whole new tactic. And this is their use of the Civil courts, not the criminal courts, which had proved useless. People were more than willing to be falsely charged, go to jail, stand trial, and be acquitted. That's what's happened. Out of four hundred cases, only two convictions. It's about like that. Hardly a conspiracy.

So instead of that they decided to use the civil courts, the big difference being, you have no resources at all, since they don't appoint you a lawyer in civil court. You have to find one and go into debt or liquidate whatever it is you own in the world, or borrow money up the butt, to have a defense for yourself.

So they took four of us and charged us then we started the People's Park Defense Union, which is an open forum. There's nobody left in the Defense Union who's an actual *member* except us. It made people run for the hills.

You can ask anybody, even today, "Are you a member of the People's Park Defense Union?" And they'll say, "Oh well, I'm not…I don't think so. Uh, what's that? Mmm…

See you later." They don't want to take a chance on being sued. Before people just attended the meetings. now people are fearful.

Here's the deal. There's no *real membership* in the People's Park Defense Union. There never was. At least, if there was, I haven't ever known anything about it. All I know is that at the time they were tearing down the Free Box we met *every day* at 5 o'clock. People were just out of their minds trying to figure what we could possibly do. And if all I could figure out to do was that four of us were gonna go off and make signs, *that's what we would do.* That's what kind of conspiracy this was, if it was a conspiracy at all.

It was just an opportunity for like-minded people to get together, and maybe even only disagree. We didn't have all that much in common, some of us. Some things you'll never resolve, like the violence versus non-violence angle. People will say, " Get out of here with that non-violence crap, Carol, because they're shooting guns at us! We're nuts if we don't defend ourselves."

Well, ... and this goes on forever. It sure *does* look like you're nuts if you don't defend yourself against bullets and so forth, but you know, I'm just damned if I'll stoop to tactics like that. That's the bind that a non-violent person gets in. And I think that some of the people who spoke for violence, spoke very well. And that's what the forum was about. It was about hearing all sides.

You know if People's Park accomplished anything, it's about trying to engender a respect for every last voice—even the voice you fear, even the voice you don't want to hear. I think that that's one thing that, as I try to count up our accomplishments, we *did* accomplish. And Rosebud was an important part of that

We did a really good job of illuminating, yes, even the most *frightening* of voices.

So, they decided to sue the People's Park Defense Union, four people, including myself, who were supposed to be key leaders. And they actually said in the complaint that we were key leaders. I find this so funny. I used to wear a little key around my neck, and drag it on the ground now and then, because I thought it was so ironic. Nobody does what I tell them to do.

So, they sued us, plus fifty Jane and John Does, and that's where the real fear came in. Because *you* could become the first or second Jane or John Doe by what? Throwing a rose in the sand? That's what got me into it. What? Meeting nightly at a cafe? That's was one of their complaints against Bob Sparks. What? Standing around the Park making speeches? That's what got David Nadel into it.

If people can be thrown into a civil suit on charges that flimsy, *anybody* can be in there. And that I think is the *power* of this thing. People turn around and think, "Oh, Can I be seen with Carol? You know? That's their excuse for calling David Nadel and myself a "conspiracy." It says literally in the complaint, "David Nadel and Carol were seen together in People's Park on numerous occasions." There's a period at the end of that sentence. That's all there is. That's it. That's why we're considered a conspiracy. Now, if anybody seen with me can be considered part of my conspiracy, you can see what happened to my guest list. You know, a lot of people disappeared. A lot of people are honestly frightened, and who can blame them?

Here I am. I have no property. I have no money. I have nothing of value except perhaps my guitar. It certainly is more valuable than my car. And I'm now between thirty and forty thousand dollars in debt to lawyers—a debt that, when you consider my income has been around poverty level all my life, will probably take, you know, two lifetimes to pay off. That's what they do when they want to stop people from speaking. I'm told that it's because I'm a persuasive speaker. I don't know. I feel like I haven't persuaded a gopher in People's Park.

You persuaded me.

But try to persuade someone who believes that there is a time for violence, to be completely non-violent. I even concede that there are times when violence can be described as "necessary," or at least you can make a really good case for it. I appreciate that. I'm not an idiot.

But, I feel as though People's Park will live or die by its own tactics. And that at People's Park, in particular, we need now to redefine the fight and take it out of the street and put into people's hearts. Because if people knew the story of all the commissions who voted *against* that development, they'd know the real violence was being done to the homeless people whose possessions were being trash-compacted. I think they would care. I think they'd find it harder to just *dismiss* the issue they way they can now. But it's a hard sell. People's Park is a very hard sell. Rosebud, the little warrior, may have died in vain.

This was the fight that went on in 1969, and it's happening all over again. But, they found a new weapon—the civil suit. They tried for criminal charges. As a matter of fact, the probably the most potent complaint against me is that I'm supposed to have attacked a volleyball player. They took me into criminal court on the charge of battery against this volleyball player. He gave a false name, and a false address. He didn't show up for the criminal trial. But that remains a complaint against me in the civil suit. When are they gonna fish this guy out of the woodwork? Will he ever give a correct name and address, so we can really talk to him about it?

The people who were, you know, not in jail the way I was, told me he was a very reluctant witness against me, and would make a police report only on condition that he never had to have anything to do with it again. At that point, I guess they felt they needed some volleyball player to complain against me. Well, I don't know. I don't know whether they'll be able to find him and use him against me. All I know is that he'll have a hard time, you know, lying the way they want him to lie in court. And that's about all they have besides the roses and the cardboard saw as against me.

I had heard that the charge against you was that you threw roses into the volleyball court and danced with a cardboard saw.

That's actually a charge against David, that he danced with a cardboard saw. I'm the one who's accused of, and did in fact, create those cardboard saws, which are just what they sound like. Yes. I cut them out of cardboard one night because each one says, "I came. I saw, I conquered" on the side, which is the phrase, "Veni. Vidi.

Vinci." I thought this was the funniest joke. And I thought people would see the point and laugh. It was like an art project.

Automatically folk in the Park would pick them up, make sawing motions, laugh, dance, and enjoy them. You couldn't cut *anything* with these cardboard saws. But apparently, the Regents are trying to characterize the cardboard as an incitement to riot, a symbol of vandalism, something like that.

You could see it as vandalism if you want to, but I think eventually this community will come to its senses and remove the volleyball courts. All they do is sit there and take up space. Nobody plays on them unless they're paid. Players have admitted that to many people I just think that they're a travesty.

I was told that U.C. students were given credit if they would go play on the courts— P. E. credit. They also had a few people getting ROTC—Military training credit. Talk about a travesty!

Yeah, the Regents don't feel it. It's the students that feel it. And I feel *for* them. I went to school there twenty odd years ago, and it was a very different place. It was still a tough place, but it was a place at least there was some thought of Free Speech left.

That's where it started.

Well, twenty years ago was right about the time when they started to eradicate any remnant of the Free Speech movement which was in '64. I was there. What they had done was pick the Movement up whole, like the

Criminology Department, pick it up entirely, and remove it from campus. They wanted to absolutely get rid of the radical thinkers. And the Criminology Department. There wasn't much they could do with "us radical" who thought, for instance, that crime was caused by poverty, and poverty was increases by racism. They just had to pretty much eliminate the department. So they did. They got rid of it.

This is exactly what Michael Rossman who was there in '68 and '69 meant. He felt that the whole issue of People's Park was an attempt to get rid of radical thinking.

You can prove it. You know at least it's easy to prove because they have to take minutes of the Regents' meetings. You can go back to 1950, and see in the Regents' meetings, that they saying things like "We're worried about the Southside campus; things are kind of outa hand down there."

The 60's culture was burgeoning. Music and poetry, all of this stuff was happening that they couldn't control. And students weren't really in charge of it. It was a sort of part student, and part non-student culture. It was its own culture. And it was happening fresh, right there on the South side of campus. Everybody was hopeful. It was vibrant.

Chapter Eighteen
Bob Remembers

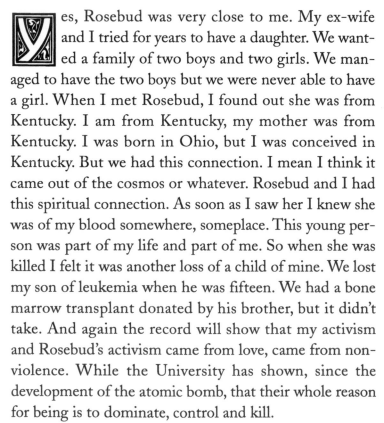

es, Rosebud was very close to me. My ex-wife and I tried for years to have a daughter. We wanted a family of two boys and two girls. We managed to have the two boys but we were never able to have a girl. When I met Rosebud, I found out she was from Kentucky. I am from Kentucky, my mother was from Kentucky. I was born in Ohio, but I was conceived in Kentucky. But we had this connection. I mean I think it came out of the cosmos or whatever. Rosebud and I had this spiritual connection. As soon as I saw her I knew she was of my blood somewhere, someplace. This young person was part of my life and part of me. So when she was killed I felt it was another loss of a child of mine. We lost my son of leukemia when he was fifteen. We had a bone marrow transplant donated by his brother, but it didn't take. And again the record will show that my activism and Rosebud's activism came from love, came from non-violence. While the University has shown, since the development of the atomic bomb, that their whole reason for being is to dominate, control and kill.

Rosebud was murdered. She was executed – a police execution. They didn't even attempt to talk to her. They didn't even attempt to get anybody there to talk to her. They didn't use a bull horn, they didn't use anything to negotiate, they didn't want to negotiate. And she was trapped, she knew she was trapped. And when she called her friend Jim Henry and said, "They're going to shoot me" she had probably heard them say, "If you find her, shoot her." Because why would she think – just being trapped in a bedroom – they would shoot her, if she had-n't heard that they were going to shoot. The other conflict in their story is that she charged the cop with a machete. But he had a dog, an attack dog, with him. Now, Oakland attack dogs are trained to attack immediately if anybody comes to their handler. So, what happened to the dog? I think they sniffed her out with the dog and the dog found her scent in that room. The officer charged and she tried to run and they shot her in the back twice. The autopsy report showed that they shot her in the back. They probably turned her around then and shot her twice.

I think she was executed with her hands handcuffed behind her back. I don't believe that Rosebud attacked anybody. But she was trapped in this place and they did-n't use negotiation or any kind of civilized manner of tak-ing her out of the house alive. First of all, I don't think that the Chancellor wanted her to come out alive. Because the next day when he was confronted on campus by the Red Ribbon man, Don, who said, "You didn't have to kill her" the Chancellor replied "She didn't have to be in my house." Rosebud was killed because she invaded the Chancellor's house. Whenever we have performed an occupation of buildings on campus (and we have done dozens) the police contact the Chancellor to give them permission to do arrests. He is the one who gives the orders. So the Chancellor standing outside his mansion on August 25 ordered his police officers to kill Rosebud. He didn't say "Don't kill Rosebud. Don't kill that young girl." He knew who she was. The police had full knowledge of who she was.

They knew her size, that she was no threat to all of the cops with their bullet proof vests, their mace, their guns and their dogs. And everybody knew that, but they did not want to save Rosebud's life, they wanted to kill her.

Their lie was that she was charging like this with both hands on the machete, that the cop was falling backwards into the bathtub and he was shooting. If so, when she was charging, first of all, where did the dog go? Why didn't the dog take her out? That's a first problem right there. The bullets that entered Rosebud's body were going down. She was hit in the trachea and the bullet went straight down into her heart. She was hit in the back; the direction was down.

If she was over the person, who was shooting her, the bullets would be going up. She was shot in the neck. If she had been over him the bullets would have gone up. That's all documented in the autopsy report.

Chapter Nineteen

The Filmmaker Remembers

OU CAN CRY IN FRONT OF ME ANDY. YOU CAN CRY IN FRONT OF ME JIM HENRY. YOU CAN CRY IN FRONT OF ME CAROL. YOU CAN CRY IN FRONT OF ME WILLIAM, I WON'T TELL ANYBODY .

WHY DID THEY SEND IN THAT PARTICULAR COP? THAT GUY HAD BEEN SHOT BY A ROBBERY SUSPECT AND WAS SCARED HIMSELF.

Don't cry Andy. Don't cry you grieving family, you grieving river.

Gone to blue skies now.

Lost twinkling eyes, lost gentle diligence. All those books to study, so much to learn.

The police version changes from day to day.

We didn't know what to do.

That evening almost two hundred of us marched in People's Park.

A few UC officials showed up. We were pissed at them, more than pissed, we were enraged. Lots of us got in their faces and told them to get out.

In a while we marched to the UC campus police station.

We chanted and yelled.

We gathered back in the park at 9PM. The cops were there full force. They were looking for people to arrest, you could smell it. The cops started in with their clubs. It was no fun.

When the cops knocked one of us unconscious, we started throwing rocks. A cop made a crack about Rosebud and her boyfriend Andy Barnum went for him. Who could blame him? But he got arrested of course, they couldn't wait. They also arrested John Vance. So much for memorial tributes. Andy's still afraid to walk near the campus. He'll always be.

A few minutes after Andy and John were arrested, a bonfire broke out on the corner of Telegraph and Haste. When a crowd of more than a hundred checked it out, the cops finally pulled back. Angry people started ripping wood from the new UC dorm being constructed at 2424 Channing and a large barricade was built and set on fire. Some of us said, let's be non violent. Some of us wanted to fight back. Andy said put a bunch of anarchists together at a meeting and its like out of the Mad Hatter's Tea Party. Where did the white rabbit go:

Let's rip it all down.

We'll land in jail too.

The whole country's still a jail baby. Ask anybody "moving on" after ten PM when they chase you out of People's Park.

Oh Rosebud, our baby before you became a socialist at five, a rebel with a cause at nine, had an angry menarche and a political agenda, and died on the cross at nineteen.

Rosebud of the soul

It was not your day.

Don't cry Andy, don't cry. Don't cry Mom and Dad, don't cry. Don't cry Teddy, don't cry.

When Andy saw the autopsy report he went bananas.

I had run to the post office and when I got back they were all in the front room, Andy and Michaela who was bright and pretty and had only one finger on each hand, William looking strangely softened, not his usual brisk sarcastic self, Rich labeling in the film room, Eighty nine year old Jim sitting huffily on the couch pulling me aside and saying, "Whatcha hanging out with them? They're a bunch of anarchists."

I'd done a little film about Jim. It was called HOW I GOT OUT OF JAIL AND RAN FOR GOVERNOR OF INDIANA and it was about his getting in the face of city marshals in the 1920s and putting back people's furniture when they were evicted and the marshals had just put it all out on the street.

So, everybody has his political agenda, me I just like to hide behind the camera where the questions get answered through the lens way before I ask them.

Like a thousand years before I ask them.

So Andy was freaking out a little on the front porch and then in the front room, which is understandable because the autopsy report was sad and weird and seemed to show that something was very different from the way the media had said it was, or quoted the cops as saying it was, that August day, almost a year before.

I was afraid Andy would go avenge Rosebud and land back in jail so I cracked out the two ten milligram libriums someone had left the day before, and after he swallowed, gave him an assignment to go look up stuff at the Library.

I broke into the chancellor's house to show them how it felt to be in a place that seemed safe, only then it would turn scary. Like the Park when the cops would come at ten thirty PM and chase us. Like the hiding place under stars that wasn't a hiding place anymore when those flashlights shone in my face. Some Native American wrote about People's Park "Your land title is covered with blood." Now their land title is covered with my blood. If the trajectory of the shots was down, not up, somebody didn't tell the truth. I guess I'm an angel now and fly over your heads with my golden wings outstretched. Why did their dog go for my throat and their bullets rip off my fingers? Why did they handcuff me when I was dead? If they'd handcuffed me when I was alive, why would the cop have been afraid, like he said. Why did he shoot me in the back? Look for me in the park. I won't be in the grove anymore, I'll be down near the platform, floating over the Concerts. My jeans and socks will be new and I'll be waiting for the people to get with it, to make things better. Whatever Tom Joad and Ma Joad said, in the Grapes of Wrath *I'll say it again. I'll say it to the wind and the wind will tell you. Don't forget me. My name was Rosebud.*

Chapter Twenty

David Remembers

was initially not comprehending, and still don't comprehend why her death was necessary. The house was completely surrounded by police officers. They had guard dogs. They had mace. They had mental health intervention services available. The chancellor had been removed from the house. His wife had been removed from the house. There was no danger to them. I believe that it was an unnecessary killing. All police departments have a standard procedure for dealing with people who they consider to be emotionally unstable and those procedures require intervention, negotiation. None of them were followed in this case. There was no reason to track her down inside the house and confront her in the manner that she was confronted. That wasn't necessary.

Part of the attitude that I perceived on the part of the establishment was that she was considered to be a dangerous person and since that label had been put on her, anything that she did which was provocative was gonna result in a response that would have been far greater than the response that might have been produced had it been someone else who was not known to the police or someone else who, um, didn't have this stigma of being considered dangerous. I'm convinced that when she went into the residence, she was not intending to kill the chancellor.

Do you think she was making a gesture as to how it felt to have one's space invaded?
Yes.

Because her own had been invaded?
Exactly, police officers constantly invaded her space in the park plus her space on the streets on wherever she happened to have to live. And that invasion was accompanied by violence. I think that by her going into the chancellor's residence she was making a statement about that.

She had an intolerance of injustice. She saw the world as being composed of good people and bad people. And the good people were the one's that wanted to tear it down and rebuild it. And the bad people were the one's who were perpetuating the injustices of the society. When I first met her she was in jail and when she got out and she was homeless. For a period of time she was living in a house in Oakland but most of the time she was homeless. I had often told Rosebud that she should stay away from situations in which she would put herself at risk of being severely injured or killed because I felt that there were police officers out there who would, given the opportunity, try to kill her.

I don't know that I can say that I remember her being happy. I can remember her being — she smiled a lot, she laughed a lot, but it was sort of in the mix of the whole tragedy that she saw around her. I can't say I ever saw her really happy in the sense of having inner peace of mind.

First of all, I think that the police exploited circumstances to their advantage. That this was not a dispassioned law enforcement situation. Therefore whether or not she actually went after the officer with a machete, as he claimed, or not is irrelevant because the situation had already deteriorated at that point to the likelihood of her being killed. They had already made their first blunders in handling the situation — which is something she should've expected they would do and I think she did, as evidenced by the note she had in her purse when they found her gym bag. In it she said she was willing to die for the park. So she went into the chancellor's office with the consciousness that she was not going to come out alive. That's also verified by the telephone call that she made to Jim Henry in which she said, " They're going to kill me."

She knew that was coming. So she decided to be a martyr. She probably felt that that would be a strong statement or legacy to leave behind that was more important than her living out her life expectancy of 70 or 80 years. I don't agree with that. I think she would have been more valuable had she stayed around. But she had absolutely no way to compromise with the society and the way that it's run. This situation had certain parallels to the Buddhist monks in Vietnam who set themselves on fire to protest the Diem regime. And what a powerful and moving force that was.

Chapter 21

Steven Remembers

was reading the New York Times in August 1992. It was a story about a young girl named Rosebud Denovo who had been shot to death in the UC Berkeley's Chancellor's Mansion, in what first appeared to be just a break-in, but after reading this substantial article, it appeared she had died trying to make some kind of political statement. I had just finished a film and I was looking around for other things to focus on and I was struck. First off, her name was Rosebud, a historically loaded term - secondly, she was coming out of a political milieu I had lived through in the 60's and 70's.

So I set out trying to find out what happened and I asked the Herald Examiner and the Chronicle in San Francisco to send me their coverage. I read their stories and they seemed oddly one-sided. They agreed that she was killed because the cops were trying to protect the chancellor. They said she was obsessed with violence. I felt myself recoiling from this because it seemed like a very biased point of view. And yet the facts of the break-in, seemed to point to some psychological problems. I was able to get to her attorney, David Beauvais, who was quoted in one of the articles in San Francisco. When David picked up the phone I said "You don't know me, and I'm sorry to call you so shortly after your client's death. This story has touched me, and I need to ask you some questions." He said "Go ahead." "Was she crazy?" I asked. Then David said something that has set me off on a seven year journey. "No, she was one of the smartest people I had ever met in my life." This statement chilled me. Within two weeks of her death I flew to Berkeley. I sat down in a restaurant with him and asked a series of questions. The more he told me, the more it seemed Rosebud was a powerful representation of what it means to be young, revolutionary, passionate, thoughtful, conscious, but in some aspects, naive, in America today. He gave me some names of people who have known her. I met Bob Sparks, I met Carol Denney, Mike Lee, Andy Barnum, and Elisa Smith. Some people thought Rosebud was a violent revolutionary, others a pacifist, a spiritualist, an atheist. It was endless. I thought it would be hard to find very much objective truth in this investigation with so many perspectives. So I went to the police. I also talked to one University spokesmen and a variety of other University officials. However, it was clear that I was someone they didn't want to talk to. Probably because I had said "I'm here to discover what there is to discover. I'm a filmmaker, and looking to understand what happened." They gave me a lot of information that not only contradicted what her friends were telling me, it even contradicted what the reports had said. I started to realize I was not going to find out the objective truth this way and went home. Then David put me in touch with Rosebud's parents in Kentucky to find out if there was some connection to Rosebud's fate that could be traced back to her family. There she had been institutionalized at the age of twelve, after a conflict with the police. There was also a history of a remarkable intellect, and I started to see a broader picture. I started to see a girl who looked around and said "There's something wrong with the culture in America." That really appealed to me. In meeting her family, I sat with two grief stricken parents. It really floored me. I was looking for cause and had my antenna up, but I couldn't find the culprit.

I found out there was an activist past in her parent's lives. They had taught her to ask questions, be curious about politics and history, and she was a voracious student of all those things. Her progressive family set the stage for her curiosity for all this stuff. She had come out of a religious activism background, the church was involved in the Civil Rights Movement, so you could see the lineage. I left Lexington with more questions than answers.

I came back and forth to Berkeley, conducted more interviews, and with the help of her attorney, made a request to the DA that they release her diaries. David Beauvais was very aggressive and they released her diaries to us. Her family elected not to pursue a wrongful death lawsuit, trying to put the tragedy behind them. Then we got the diaries. We didn't get all the diaries since the Oakland Police department offered up incomplete documents. All the pages were numbered and all the notebooks were identified. There were five, maybe six notebooks. There would be notebook E, and the pages were numbered E one through E eleven, notebook

C had thirty pages in front. Everything was numbered and lot s on numbers were missing.

Anyway, these diaries showed a passionate young revolutionary spirit wrestling with ideas. From Hegel to Marx to Emma Goldman. She was trying to build a political awareness and reading everything she could get her hands on. As she was evolving this ideology of hers, the pieces and fragments were showing up in her diary. When I read it, all of a sudden her voice started to emerge. So I got her diaries and put them in a box. Then I left Berkeley and delivered them to her parents in Kentucky. I told them "Here are the materials the police didn't want to release. My heart's in the right place, I would like very much to explore this event.

I'm not making a documentary. Claire Burch did that already. I'm sitting here trying to adjust to the fact that to this day I feel she was murdered. A nineteen year old with a knife, (If she had a knife, which I have never seen, which they never showed us), entered a house with a whole lot of equipment, alarms, etc. The Chancellor and his wife had been removed from the house. At the time of Rosebud's death the house was empty. She went in there alive and she came out dead. There's the truth in her life.

I have been through this long painful process of exploration and revelation around what happened. Knowing I will never get to the whole truth, it has changed me. I used to ask the question "What's truth to me?" Now I ask the question, "Should I integrate my own struggle as well?" It has been seven years and I'm still dancing around the issue.

The experience has been very profound. This little girl reminds me of what I felt like when I was her age. Very strong. I didn't take it as far but I took a lot of chances. I didn't have her experience but I did have similar resonant experiences. I've been able to revisit my own passions. I have only my own point of view. I suspect she was surprised to find herself in a situation where her life was at stake. I don't think she was forced into that house by anybody, but I don't think she went in there expecting it would end the way it did. In that lies a remarkable tragedy.

She was a young person who saw the suffering around her and wanted to do something about it. Unfortunately, the scenario that unfolded in her own life killed her. That instinct to see the homeless and not look away, to see injustice and want to do something about it, is a very sacred one.

We are living in a culture where we are being watched. Rosebud fought for People's Park, in Berkeley, as an idea, a dream if you will. She thought of public spaces as the site for collective action. Union Square in New York City is a great historical example. Emma Goldman stood there and gave speeches seventy-five years ago. If you look at Lincoln Park in Chicago, which Rosebud visited, that was a public space where history turned a little in 1968.

Rosebud was very aware of the meaningfulness of public space, and People's Park was yet another representation of that for her. It continues to exist in Berkeley as a very loaded question mark, full of contrary opinions. In some way she connected with that energy of getting people together, doing progressive actions to affect some change. She did that in her life as a child and a s a teenager. She was very active in Kentucky, in and around her church and other places. She went to Berkeley thinking, "Oh, here is a symbol, we can rally people around this." That symbol, is still potent. I walked into People's Park having never been there until 1992 and felt the intense energy of people's dreams. I don't pass myself off as mystical, but you walk into this park and you feel something. I suspect this young girl walked into People's Park and thought, "Now this is the spot. This is where I can fight back." I think that's what happened to her.

Tragically, her passion for change killed her. I elaborate on the reason; there are a lot of ways to be killed in our culture. You can rob people, cheat, steal. Her thing was about trying to stimulate some form of consciousness in people who didn't care too much to have their consciousness stimulated. I'm not sitting in judgement; I have my own daily battle with apathy.

I think we should all think for awhile about what it means to care. That's all I think Rosebud meant finally.

Steven Starr
1999

Chapter 22

Teddy Remembers More

his is a memory from the time Rosebud and I first met: the Holiday Season 1990/1991. Rosebud and I were walking on campus. Even though it was a particularly cold winter that year, Berkeley campus was still lush with evergreens and blooming vines, and ivies with shiny leaves that climbed the gray stone of the older buildings with their terracotta roofs. The sheer abundance of the place was still happily amazing to Rosebud, as we walked along the eucalypti grove, the tall trees with their hairy peeling trunks forming a jungle line at the edge of campus, their aromatic leaves mentholating any breeze.

Rosebud was asking me what I did before I met and joined the Flea Collective. I explained that after I graduated from Xavier High School, I entered St. Andrew's-on-Hudson, the Jesuit novitiate in Poughkeepsie, N.Y. After leaving there, I bounced around from school to school, disillusioned, lonely, isolated and pretty much lost. My only political activity at this time was with the Catholic Peace Fellowship, until I met the people who were forming the Flea Collective.

"What happened?" she asked then. "I mean to the young Catholic activist?" At the age of seventeen, the news of how lives turned out the way they did gripped her like a thriller.

"What happened?" I asked myself. We were walking up toward Sproul Plaza. In front of us, the brass-colored hills behind campus, waiting for the rainy season to begin, looked burned to acres of straw, broken now and then by houses, buildings and an occasional solitary live oak looking as if it had been placed there to accommodate a hanging.

"My Lai happened. MLK was assassinated." I answered at last. "But even more so in terms of my life, Harlem happened. That was the intervening force,"

"Did you lose your faith?" she asked casually, as someone who'd never believed much. We were approaching Sather Gate.

"You know," I answered, "every once in a while, I run into someone who says, 'How can you claim that spirituality has any common ground with Marxism or Anarchism, which recognize only a material world? But that isn't what they teach. Do you think Che wasn't spiritual? That Mao or Marx didn't believe in- indeed revere- the life of the spirit? The revolutionary believes that the spirit can only find expression in this material world and, in Harlem, I can to understand that point of view.

"In 1962, I began tutoring children in Harlem, after school, as part of a program in which Xavier High School was involved. My awareness of the problems of black people both in the northern ghettos and in the southern states was born and grew. In 1964, when the Civil Rights Act was passed, I felt ecstatic. I felt that years, decades of good hearted efforts had been vindicated, that the world was finally changed. And you know, four years later, in the beginning months of 1968, I went back up to Harlem and not a thing was better for those folks. A lot of things were worse. Oh, there was some talk of change when I asked. But I had to wonder.

"And I wrestled with myself. I struggled. I would look at those kids and wonder, 'How do I say to you, after all this work, after this great triumph, how can I say to you that it will be no better in your lifetime? How do I, where do I derive the right to tell you to wait?'

"You see, I couldn't really comfort myself with hopes for future generations, because this meant accepting the misery I saw now. And I couldn't agree to the sop of the religious, "heaven" because after all, it wasn't just the Kingdom of Heaven that Jesus said the meek would have- he said they would inherit this earth. Was he merely taunting them? So, that was the question, you see: How do I temporize with this generation? What mandate of law, of God- where in anyone's teachings, Christ's, or Marx's, or Bakunian's, where does it explain how a government derives the moral authority to tell the poor to languish in squalor, to wait and wait for the earth that is theirs while it is consumed by the rich? What happened to me, Rosebud, was that my faith, or my conscience, or my moral sensibility told me that there is no logic to this life but revolution."

We were by Ludwig's Fountain as I finished my tale. Rosebud's eyes were wide with compassion as she held me and comforted me.

I regarded Rosebud as the most together person I'd ever known, thoroughly and enviably adult despite her young age. She was poised and rigorously logical in all circumstances, while maintaining a warm, frank manner. She was quick to laugh at jokes, better at making them, easy with strangers, kind to street people and their dogs. I figure that my principal contribution to her, aside from my complete and total love, was to add a calming element to her life which, at times, was too full of molten and combustible emotions that seemed to defy both her understanding and mine. She was inclined to manic spells, isolated periods of zombie-like staring, as well as adolescent attachments: writers, clothes that were one week's passion and then never spoken of again. Sometimes she was touchy: criticisms, disagreements could make her funky and combative with others, even with me. I would sometimes study her notebooks when she wasn't around, or inspect the marginalia in the books she read, the passages she highlighted. What was I to make of that exclamation point? What insight made her write "I see"?

In the early part of 1992, the winter and spring, when Rosebud and I lived together at the Info Cafe, Rosebud was reading a great deal of Philosophy. Poor Chris Del Vecchio, our roommate and best friend at the house, who also died tragically young and violently, had an impressive philosophical library which Rosebud was voraciously devouring. Then periods would set in which she declared it all a waste of time. "It's real things, doing things I admire," she said, "not talking about them."

Often enough, as a means of encouraging her, I asked her to digest her reading for me, like a mother bird chewing and feeding this heavy stuff to me in lightweight bits.

I remember Rosebud's becoming excited about a philosopher named Brentano who taught that consciousness was, at root, images shorn of all abstractions. She saw him as the unsuspected bridge between the depth psychologists, like Freud, and the existentialists, like Sartre. In this connection she was reading the nineteenth-century German philosophers. One of her passing fixations was a term – from Nietzsche, I think – "traumhaft", a sense that all beliefs – religion, love, the golden rule – were but a dream with no provable justification in morality or science. Our lives, Nietzsche claimed, our customs, were really no more than rote learning. We were, he said, actually afloat within sensation and otherwise unanchored, free but terrified, like astronauts who have left their capsule and stand in space.

"Get it?", Rosebud asked. It was Sunday and we were, as was often the case on Sundays, in bed, in the bedroom Chris Del Vecchio had given up to us so that we could have some privacy. Neither of us dressed all day. We ate brunch and even dinner on the Goodwill mattress on the floor. When she dozed, I took up the sections she'd been reading. In the afternoons, Rosebud moved on to her books.

"Heavy," I answered. "Very heavy. But bullshit."

"Why is it bullshit, baby?"

"Cause that's not how it is. Not for me. I mean, all this raging volcanic shit I feel? Everything's connected to everything else. I'm not floating. Not hardly. Are you?"

There was a round window, like a porthole, in our bedroom. It's existence had seemed a typically pointless Victorian frill until the night that the full moon had appeared there and filled the room with light so ghostly, but intense I'd found it difficult to sleep. Lost in reflection, Rosebud looked in that direction now.

"That's what I feel," she said. "A lot."

"Traumhaft?"

"Traumhaft." There are times when I wonder. Do you know Descartes? Sometimes I wonder about everybody else. Like Descartes did. How do I know "they" are not in my imagination? How do I know for sure there's anything besides me? And even so, I wonder if I can really reach what's outside of me. There seems such a terrible abyss. Even between what I feel and what I can say about it.

I've had an insight into Rosebud's and my behavior. This is something we had in common and should I think, be put into the record: we both needed to take risks. Not only because confronting the fear and ACTING provided the rites of initiation necessary for constructive personal growth as REVOLUTIONARIES, but also, on a deeper level, we both had a longing for the ecstatic clarity, the emptiness that came with facing danger. And sometimes, when we talked about the epiphanies of taking risks, how it beat the hell out of the endless grinding boredom of poverty and oppression, I wondered if the high hasn't become an addiction of us both- a heightened craving for the neuropeptide rush, an increasing temptation to raise the stakes each time, to linger a bit longer on the brink.

Anyway, I resist all Freudian explanations, which make me vaguely ill. Reality is always both more straightforward and more mysterious, more elegant, more pathetic.

"Five Things Worse Than Dying", which are:

1- Being just a meat machine, a fucking monkey body, like you're trapped inside of it, it does what it does whether you want it to or not.

2- Losing your sense of what a human being is, what they're capable of, what the word "human" even means and so not having any idea what you are or where you belong.

3- Living life but not being able to feel it because it's either not enough or it's too much (sometimes simultaneously).

4- Being so alone, you're not sure other people are real.

5- Going through life never sure what's inside your mind or what's in the world outside you.

I am 52 years old and have been utterly alienated from the American society and system my entire adult life. The last 20 years I have been in and out of jail and prison, for petty property crimes. If one looks on the Social Security Computer under my name, one will find that I was employed for 2 months in 1967, 4 months in 1995, and otherwise, not at all. If this is not concrete proof of my inability to deal with a system I find essentially evil, I do not know what is.

Here are Rosebud's last letters to me.

4-15

Teddy—

Bae. Writing you here just in case you haven't been transferred. Just got your 2nd letter.

I love you. I miss you and I'm not going to leave you. Hope your time is short.

As far as my legal situation goes I haven't even been offered a deal. I'm not sure what's going to happen.

My lawyer won't go out to pick up the money but Dave Linn says he will. He wants to know how you go about singing money over from San Quentin and from work furlough so he doesn't have to make an unnecessary trip. Please let me know. Nothing much new. Once again, I love you and miss you Bae.

Rosebud

P.S. Write back.

This letter has been recreated for readability. The original is handwritten.

4-15

Teddy—

Bro, Sorry for not writing for so long just moved out of the hole and things have been slightly crazy. I'm tired and stressed out & I wish you could be here to help me deal with this shit. Anyway please start writing me at Dan's. I haven't gotten ahold of him yet to make sure it's ok but I don't think he'll mind. I'll make sure when I get a chance.

Dave Linn's been dragging his feet about getting the money. Unfortunately it's probably too late to go around him. I finally called San Quentin myself to try and track it down and they told me the money from both places had been transferred to Susanville. Please find out if there's a way it can be released from here and if you need to fill out any more forms.

You're right about one thing — most people around here are full of shit.

Miss you. Wondering when this fun of bad luck will end. Aside from everything else, quarter meal has run out of something (once the main course and once vegetables)

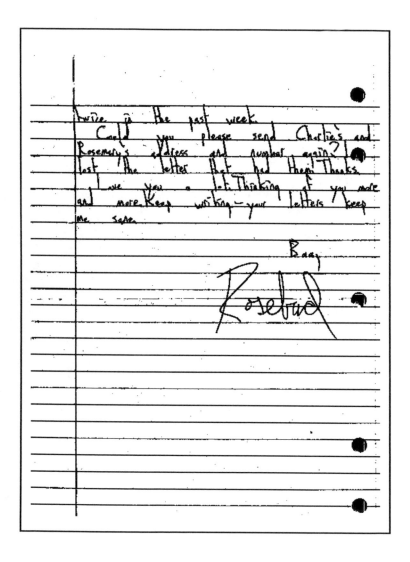

4-22

Teddy—

Bug—Got letters from you today and yesterday. Still love you and miss you. Great news about Charlie —I'm psyched. Will make that call as soon as I have money to do so — I'm really broke at the moment. I don't even have money to buy stamps.

I read about Halfus in the paper. It is really being hyped. Demonstration in the park on Sun. Our friend Lani is going to be there. Things could get interesting.

Not much else is happening. Just making time til you get out. Still no luck finding a lawyer. I'll keep trying. Bug.

Rosetrie

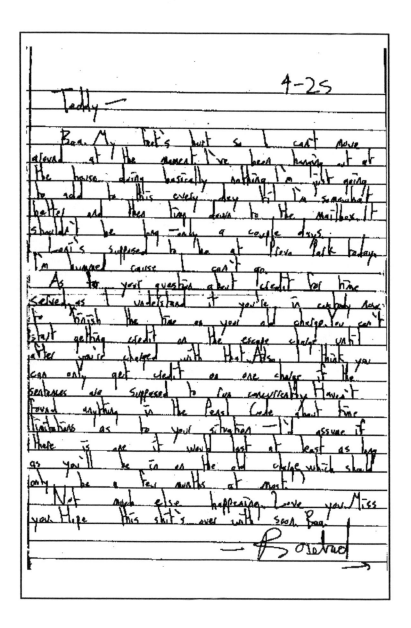

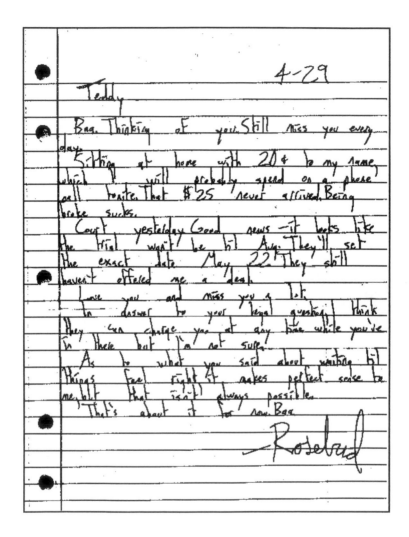

4-29

Teddy,

Bag. Thinking of you. Still miss you every day. Sitting at home with 20¢ to my name, which I will probably spend on a phone call tonite. That $25 never arrived. Being broke sucks.

Court yesterday. Good news — it looks like the trial won't be til Aug. They'll set the exact date May 22. They still haven't offered me a deal.

Love you and miss you a lot.

In answer to your legal question, I think they can charge you at any time while you're in there, but I'm not sure.

As to what you said about waiting til things feel right, it makes perfect sense to me, but that isn't always possible.

That's about it for now. Bag

Rosebud

6-17-92

Teddy —

Dave Lien told me you were in Santa Rita. I wrote you a couple of times at Susanville. Anyway I'm o.k. and I'm sorry it took so long for me to write you. I didn't realize how long it had been — the days are starting to blur together. Loving you and missing you all the time. Can't wait for you to get out so we can be together and get things done.

In case I haven't told you yet my trial date is Sept. 14. Kind of nervous about it. Organizing a couple of concerts in People's Park a few weeks from now. They should be pretty cool. I'll let you know how it goes.

The national political scene is pretty much calm altho there's a lot of tension in the air. The elections are going to be interesting. If Perot wins, the shit could really hit the fan. I don't think he has much chance tho. Not much else to say. Sick of the same old scene. Miss you! Ben

Love you always,

Rosebud

6-26-92

Teddy

Baa, Working nonstop to organize this concert on the 27th. Haven't had time to breathe. I'll write you with all the details after it happens.

Demonstrating in San Francisco today to free the people arrested in the Rodney King riots.

Hanging out with a dude named Jim who's helping me organize this concert. He shares a lot of our ideas I want you to meet him. (Of course he knows we're together and I'm not interested in going out with anyone but you.)

Hoping for a letter from you soon.

Love you and miss you a lot!

Let me know when your court dates are and if there's a way you can call me. Also let me know what's going on with the $240.

I'm getting sick of this town. It's not the same as it was even last year.

That's about it Baa.)

→ another piece of abstract art

BAA

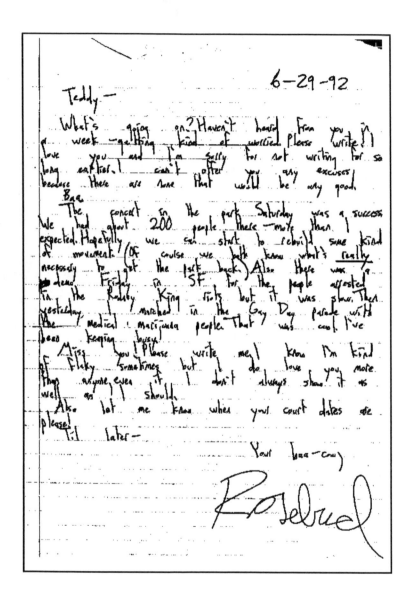

Teddy—

What's going on? Haven't heard from you in
a week—getting kind of worried please write. I
love you and I'm sorry for not writing for so
long earlier. I can't offer you any excuses
because there are none that will be any good.
Baa.

The concert in the park Saturday was a success.
We had about 200 people there—more than I
expected. Hopefully we can start to rebuild some kind
of movement. (Of course we both know what's really
necessary to get the park back.) Also there was a
dead Friday in SF for the people affected
in the Rodney King riots but it was slow. Then
yesterday I marched in the Gay Day parade with
the Medical Marijuana people. That was cool. I've
been keeping busy.

Miss you! Please write me. I know I'm kind
of flaky sometimes but I do love you more
than anyone ever if I don't always show it as
well as I should.

Also let me know when your court dates are
please. Til later—

                    Your baa-cow)

                    Rosebud

7-2-92

Teddy —

Ben. What's going on? Still haven't heard from you —
hope everything's okay. Love you, miss you, counting the
days til you get out.
   Thinking of writing a book about my political
philosophy. The other concert may happen, after all but it
will probably be low-key. Also I'm working on
organizing a class-action lawsuit on behalf of the
People's Park protesters.
   My parents are visiting SF next week. They'll
probably take me out to dinner. Wish you could meet
them. I wonder what they'd make of you.
   Ben.
   Let me know what's going on with (1) your
court dates and (2) the $240.
   That's about it.

                    Your ben-cony

                    Rosebud

7-14-92

Tebby—

Sending you a $10 money order. Make sure it g
on your books. Also sending a letter in another
envelope. Love you

Bay

Rosebud

7-14-92

Teddy —

Sorry for not writing for so long. I ran out of stamped envelopes and it took me awhile to get to the post office to get more. Spent some of the money you sent me on a whole bunch of envelopes + stamps though, so now I'll be able to write you all the time.

My parents were visiting SF this week, hung out with them and ate a lot of real food. It was cool. They are still liberals but they've adjusted to having a daughter who's an anarchist. (I don't know what they'd make of you tho — one of these days I'll have to introduce you to them.)

The political scene is pretty quiet right now. That's about it. Still love you and miss you. Thanks for sending me your card. I'll be there. Bang

Rosebud

7-25-92

Teddy—

I Have a cold. I've been sleeping a lot lately. I hope I got over it soon. Good to see you Thursday. It made me miss you more than I love you a lot! Baa! Pigs have been all over the avenue lately. It's making me paranoid even tho they don't have anything on me. Looks like the shit with the parks getting started up again then on top of that, the US may be sleeping Son of Desert Storm. I hate the government! Baa.

That's about it. Looking forward to finally being with you.

Your baa-cow,

Rosebud

7-29-92

Teddy—

Ban,

Anniversary of the volleyball courts being put in
is coming up. There's going to be a demonstration
That should be interesting.

Otherwise not much is happening. I'm finally over
my cold. Still love and miss you.

Not hanging out with Jim as much anymore
altho I still want you to meet him. DON'T
WORRY—he knows I'm your old lady and I am
not at all interested in anyone else. This is a
strictly political thing.

Ban!

Can't wait to see you again. When is your exact
release date?

Nervous about my trials. I'm trying not to think
about it much except when I have to. I can't
wait til all this shit is over.

That's about it for now...

Yours always,

Rose

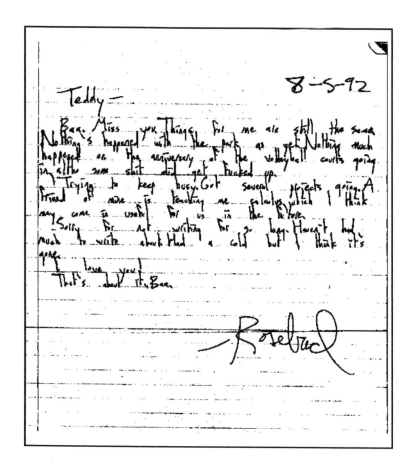

People's Park Chronology
1957-1997

June 22, 1957

The regents of the University of California allocated the sum of 1.3 million dollars (which included students funds) for the purchase of land in the South Campus area. This was part of the University's "master plan" – developing city land for the use of the University. Part of the land in this package was the site later to become People's Park.

February, 1968

All residents of the area were evicted, the houses demolished and the lot left empty. Due to financial constraints actual building on the lot was postponed by the University.

April 13, 1969

The vacant site (bounded by Telegraph Avenue and Bowditch and by Dwight and Haste) becomes a parking lot and a blemish on the landscape as it fills with abandoned cars and trash. Residents and local store owners gather to discuss alternative uses for the space. Local merchant and activist Mike Delacour proposed a user-developed and maintained park. This idea had been advanced earlier by the University's committee on Housing and Environment.

April 20, 1969

An article appearing in the local alternative paper, the Berkeley Barb, encouraging the creation of a park, brings several hundred people to the lot. Together they plan to clear and level the ground, plant flowers, grass and trees. Local merchants contribute equipment and the more serious machinery is rented with the help of donations collected from local residents. A playground and swings are set up for the children and by evening a communal cooking area is already distributing free food to all participants.

April 30, 1969

"Creative control" over a quarter of the land is promised to supporters of the park in a meeting with Executive Vice Chancellor Cheit, who also guaranteed that no university construction would start without advanced warning. Two days prior to the meeting he had announced his plans of building an intramural soccer field in the park in the near future, should the finances be available.

May 6. 1969

Representatives of People's Park committee, ASUC senators and members of the college of environmental design met with Chancellor Roger Heyns, and were given three weeks to form a joint committee and submit a plan for the construction of a park.

May 7, 1969

Vice Chancellor Cheit denied that the university was to begin construction on the next Thursday. He repeated his guarantee that UC would give warning prior to the actual construction.

May 8, 1969

Chancellor Heyns met with joint committee members Sim Van der Ryn (chairman of the Chancellor's committee of housing and environment), ASUC Senator Bachrach and Wendy Schlessinger of the Peoples Park Committee to discuss the devising of a plan for the park under Van der Ryn. It was understood that the plans were subject to review by university regents and that Chancellor Heyns had full veto powers.

May 1, 1969

While Chancellor Heyns' was out of Berkeley for a speaking engagement, his office issued a release stating that the university would "...have to put up a fence to reestablish the conveniently forgotten fact that the field is indeed the University's. The release further stated that the university is now prepared to proceed with site development. This property at (Bowditch, Haste, and Dwight) belongs to the Regents of the University of California and will not be available to unauthorized persons". The chancellor blamed these actions on the failure of the individuals working on the land to form a "responsible committee" for the university to consult with, and refusal to discontinue user development of the land. However in an earlier letter Van der Ryn of the university's Housing and Developing Committee stated that the workers in the park had showed "good faith" by discontinuing development of the disputed land.

May 14, 1969

In the middle of the night fifty one "no trespassing" signs were posted around the park by university work-men and Berkeley Police. Later that same day park sup-porters gathered to organize a series of protests against the university' plans. An eleven-member negotiating committee was set up, aiming to reach a settlement on the park.

May 15, 1969

A "state of emergency" which remained since the Third World Strike at the University the previous February, enabled two hundred and fifty Highway Patrol and Berkeley law enforcement officers to seize control over the Peoples Park area. Armed with rifles and tear gas and dressed in bulletproof "flak jackets" they cleared the park and closed off an eight-block area . Under this heavy guard an eight-foot steel mesh fence was con-structed around the park. At 10 a.m. a resolution was passed that requested the designation of a portion of the land known as Peoples Park as the "Environmental Design field station". At noon it was announced that there was to be a rally on the steps of Sproul Hall on the University campus.

ASUC president-elect Dan Siegel spoke at the rally and discussed possible strategies against the university's actions. One of the options he proposed was to peacefully return to the park in protest. A chant arose from the crowd - "We want the park" and together approximately six thousand people began to march down the three blocks separating the rally venue from the park site.

While the crowd stood chanting and singing. a demonstrator opened a fire hydrant. As the police moved in to turn it off rocks were thrown at them. They retaliated by firing tear gas, in an attempt to disperse the crowd.

The situation quickly escalated to a "street battle", demonstrators launching rock and missiles at the police while the south campus area was being flooded with tear gas. A city owned car was overturned and burned by demonstrators.

A special squad of Sheriff's deputies armed with shotguns proceeded down the streets of Berkeley firing into crowds and even at individuals. Although they began by using bird shot, they later moved into using double-O buckshot . apparently because that was the only thing left. Many demonstrators were seriously wounded, including Allen Blanchard who was permanently blinded. Demonstrator James Rector was killed by police fire.

The police slowly cleared the area around the park and campus by using small armed groups, and a National Guard gas unit roving the back streets in an army jeep with a police shotgun guard.

By 5:30 the violence had subsided. At 9:00 P.M. a curfew was imposed and a ban on public assembly was imposed. Governor Reagan, based on the request of Berkeley City Officials, activated the National Guard and three battalions of the 49th Infantry Brigade.

By the end of the day seven hundred and ninety one policemen from the City of Berkeley, the Highway Patrol, and nine bay area communities, had been deployed in Berkeley. Forty eight people were arrested.

At least one hundred and twenty eight people, among them three reporters, were injured and reported to public hospitals. There were many gunshot wounds, of which twelve cases required immediate hospitalization. Nineteen policemen were treated for injuries, none were actually hospitalized.

May 16, 1969

Berkeley was invaded by the National Guard. Police broke up an attempted rally on Sproul Hall steps. Three thousand people marched to the downtown Shattuck shopping area of Berkeley protesting police brutality and deployment of the National Guard. The National Guard dispersed the march and a meeting to plan demonstration tactics was broken up with tear gas. Twenty one participants were arrested.

A "peaceful takeover" of downtown Berkeley was voted on in nearby Oakland because of the Berkeley curfew by two thousand people. Their goal was to "make certain that no normal business goes on in the city while there are troops"and to insist that the National Guard be withdrawn.

May 17-19, 1969

Throughout the city large numbers of demonstrators gathered but were dispersed by the police and the National Guard. At the same time attempts to start other "Peoples Park Annexes" were stopped by the police and National Guard who followed the march and effectively uprooted anything that was planted.

On the 19th at 10:12 P.M. James Rector died of massive injuries to his lower body.

May 20, 1969

The Faculty of UC conducted a memorial for James Rector at Sproul Hall. It was attended by nearly four thousand people However when the people who had attended, attempted to leave , guardsmen blocked the way. After the crown had moved to the Chancellor's mansion, local police broke up the crowd with clubs and tear gas.Afterwards on the main plaza a referendum about decisions re the park, was voted on. The people were then told that"chemical agents were going to be dropped" They felt trapped when an army helicopter flew over the area, dropping CS tear gas, a type outlawed for use by the Geneva Convention. Many of the students and demonstrators vomited and became severely sick. The CS tear gas floated into the community and caused illness among children playing in Strawberry . It also floated into Cowell Hospital, causing further illness among patients.

Berkeley City Council called a special meeting to discuss solutions to the situation. One suggestion made by Mayor Wallace Johnson was that a "Neighborhood Park" be erected at the site of Peoples Park, on the basis of a lease of the land by the University to the City.

Finally the council called for a County Grand Jury investigation of the violence of the past week.

May 22, 1969

Local police and the National Guard arrested 482 people, charging them with blocking the street and failure to disperse after sealing off six blocks of downtown Berkeley. Those arrested were taken to Santa Rita Prison, where the average bail per person was set at $800.

The University's referendum on People's Park boasted the largest voter turnout in the University's history. The released results revealed that of the 14,969 who voted, 12,719 wanted to keep the park.

May 23, 1969

A motion to take down the fence around People's Park and investigate police activities was voted for by the Faculty Senate by a landslide of 642 to 95.

After a front page story in the San Francisco *Chronicle* accused Santa Rita Prison guards of mistreating the prisoners, a court restraining order was put into effect to prevent further misconduct. Disciplinary action was said to have been taken against the guards.

May 24-29, 1969

During this period, alternative "annex" parks were set up in unoccupied lots around Berkeley, the largest of which was People's Park Annex #1. Meanwhile, protests and arrests by police continued to occur daily.

A nonviolent protest march of 9,000 students from around California walked from Sacramento to the State Capitol on May 26.

The Academic Senate of the University voted to remove part of the fence around People's Park in time for a march in support of the park set for Memorial Day. On May 27, the Regents were asked to permit a "community generated park" by the Berkeley City Council.

The City Council announced its readiness to lease a part of the park for a "user-developed, user-maintained park" after Chancellor Roger Heyns decided to lease the eastern 200 feet to the City of Berkeley on May 29. The police were made ready for potential up-risings.

May 30, 1969

A five mile march through the Berkeley streets and into People's Park results in no violence. An estimated 20,-30,000 people participate.

June 20, 1969

Guarded by twenty-four hour security, the People's Park is now a 270 x 465 foot grass and asphalt lot enclosed by an eight foot steel fence. The Regents of the University of California have voted to turn People's Park into a soccer field and parking lot.

May 8, 1972

Anti-war demonstrators tear down fence in protest over Nixon's mining of Hai Phone Harbor and invading Cambodia. Mutual aid police departments are called in a and tear gas is used to disperse crowds, gas drafts into apartments and homes causing sickness and respiratory problems for small children and the elderly.

1974

Community activists establish a base from which to organize the support and defense of the park directly across the street at 2501 Hillegass.

1974 to 1979

This community provides lifestyle support services to the occupants of People's Park (showers, food, legal assistance, sanctuary, political library, lounge and temporary short-term shelter).

1974

A student-register group, sponsored by SAUCE called the People's Park Project/Native Plant Forum is formed to negotiate garden and planting projects with U.C. It takes this group three years to negotiate the placement of one bench in the Park.

1976

A large rally on Sproul Plaza to promote the National Continental Walk for disarmament and Social Justice marches to and through People's Park in recognition of its role in the anti-war and social justice movement. This walk had started in Ukiah and ended nine months later in Washington D.C. People's Park is represented throughout this national march by several Park activists.

1977

In protest of the U.S. Government's attempts to ignore the treaties of U.S. native lands and exploit their resources, a community activist conducts a forty day fast in People's Park. This protest is supported by the American Indian Movement (AIM) and has official permission from CU administration.

1978

Community activists, students, neighborhood residents, street people and some merchants and church people form the People's Park Council to act as the community's eyes, ears and voice for People's Park. Its charter entitles it to deal with the day to day activities, events, gardening and defense of the Park. It is also the whistle blower whenever U.C. starts talking development. The P.P.C. negotiate construction of the People's Stage.

1978 Christmas

U.C., knowing it is going to begin development of a fee parking lot on the West End of People's Park, begin a covert campaign to evict the People's Park/homeless activists from their base-camp on the campus of the American Baptist Seminary of the West (ABSW). The People's Park Council thwart the initial attempts by putting out an embarrassing leaflet accusing ABSW of evicting this community at Christmas time while its members are out of the state arranging a bone marrow transplant for one of its children who had leukemia. ABSW delays the eviction proceedings, (initiated by and paid for by UC) until the group returns home to defend itself in court.

1979

U.C. starts talking about development of a student only fee lot. They pretend to allow P.P. to "user-develop" the West End parking lot. By allowing Park workers to fill pot-holes, clean up trash and debris, and plant landscaping around the lot. U.C. assumes P.P.C. will allow it to "resurface" the lot. After all, P.P.C. has its stage. What more can it want? Under an agreement, U.C. recognizes that the parking lot is a part of People's Park.

April 1979

One week after the death of the young leukemia victim, ABSW (with attorneys hired by UC) issues a 30-day eviction notice. An eight-month legal battle ensues, during which time the People's Park Council and the Community Group agree and voluntarily move out of the offices and community rooms at 2501 Hillegass. While this is a blow to the effectiveness of these two groups, it is thought the legal battle for the house at 2529 Hillegass can be won. The activist group has an oral/written contract with ABSW to restore the house after it was severely damaged by a fire in 1975.

Fall 1979

U.C. paves the West End with asphalt, paints parking stripes, installs concrete wheel stops and two brand new shiny red ticket machines. Park activists are arrested in Park for observing all this and protesting. A rally is held at Sproul Plaza with about 25 Park regulars. A string of balloons is displayed and people are told this is going to be the barricade for the grand opening of the lot the next morning. This march goes down the corner of Telegraph with the People's Park banner and the chain of balloons. On arriving at the Park the balloons are tied across the Haste Street entrance. The march down Telegraph had gathered 50-75 people. A vigil is established on the West End and "Boycott This Lot" signs are made. Through the evening about one hundred and fifty people gather to vigil, continue the picket and play music.

November 1979

A Berkeley judge (newly appointed) with a previous bias toward hippie types and unrepentant radicals, orders the group evicted after illegally denying a petition for time to hire a new lawyer. This puts 22 men, women, infants, teenagers and disabled persons out their home of five years. UC had struck another blow against opponents of its expansion into the south side neighborhood. UC now dominates most of the ABSW campus. Out of this assault on an activist stronghold , Berkeley's homeless and housing rights movement is formed. The city later orders this Berkeley Historic Landmark demolished so ABSW could have a parking lot.

November 15, 1979 5:00am

U.C. police in riot gear, Berkeley cops and Mayor Gus
Newport show up. Newport tells the Berkeley police to
leave, this is not their jurisdiction. Some Berkeley police
say the mayor is not their boss and they will stay if they
want to. Demonstrations continue to block the two entrances to the East lot and most students refuse to use the
lot. "Park at your own risk" and "Free lot not fee lot" signs
are erected. Through the morning the crowd grows and
the mayor meets with the chancellor. To avoid a violent
confrontation, the chancellor calls for a "cooling off" period at which time U.C. will "re-evaluate" its parking lot
plan. Holes begin appearing in the newly-paved lot. By
evening it is decided to do an occupation of the lot. Work
continues through the day and by late evening the brand
new blue and gold CU signs and the shiny red ticket machines are buried, bent and mutilated, under mounds of
asphalt being dumped on both sides of the lot. Some re-
ferred to this growing wall as "tank traps". The workers
use the concrete wheel stops to outline new paths
through the West End. By dark, over 25 species of green-
ery have been planted. One contingent of gardeners pays
a secret visit to the chancellor's home on campus and
selects several choice plants from his beautiful garden and
greenhouse. The occupation lasts a month.

Throughout the 70s

People continue to bring trees, shrubs, flowers, plants
and seeds to plant in People's Park. Annual celebrations
and commemorations of the month-long anniversary of
the Park (April 20-May 19) include rallies, marches, can-

dlelight vigils, picnics, barbeques, potlucks, work parties and be-ins. Street vendors use site for their morning space lottery.

June 14, 1980

UC police pull the power cord on a concert and the crowd takes the party to the intersection of Haste and Telegraph. The group that was cut off, an African Dance and drum troupe, takes their performance to the intersection and entertains the protesters. Some People's Park activists remain in the Park to watch band and sound equipment and are caught in a UC police sweep through the Park in riot gear, clubbing people indiscriminately even those just sitting on lots. One man is clubbed in the ribs and laid up with cracked ribs for several weeks. As evening comes on,trash fires are started and Telegraph remains closed until early A.M. City officials decide to just let it fizzle out on its own. At the next city council meeting, the mayor criticizes UC for its handling of an otherwise peaceful and joyous event.

Summer 1980

Community activists, students, merchants, church people and homeless start talking about forming a land trust for People's Park.

December 14, 1980

Over a hundred people gather to observe the worldwide call of Yoko Ono for several minutes of silence in honor of John Lennon.

January 1981

A non-profit land conservancy for P.P. is registered with the state and has a non-profit tax-exempt status.

March 28, 1981

Park and Community activists organize an anti-nuke rally and march against UC's TRICA MK III nuclear reactor. The occasion is the second anniversary of the Three Mile Island disaster. Berkeley City cops organize a special squad of tactical forces to try and stop the marchers as they leave the Park on Haste St. The cop in charge says the march can only continue on the sidewalk. The banner carriers agree and the crowd slowly moves toward the side walk. As soon as it reaches Telegraph it flows back into the middle of the street. The police make no attempts to stop the march and it continues through the middle of campus to the nuclear reactor on the north side. Two People's Park activists are later charged and convicted (by the same judge that had evicted the community house) of littering because they had thrown organic waste on the roof of the reactor.

December 14, 1981 & 1982

UC stops planned events for a memorial to John Lennon. Police in riot gear prevent sound equipment from being brought into the Park. Street people organize a pot and pan and oil drum jam session and beat out rhythms for hours until all of the makeshift drums are beyond recognition. Later, neighbors complain that they would rather have had to listen to the amplified music than that incessant banging.

December 1982
UC begins holding what it calls the People's Park community planning meetings.

Summer 1984
The director of the California School of the Deaf donates playground equipment to the park. Park workers remove it from the school site and install it on the east end of the Park. For nearly two weeks, community children and adults play on the structure. U.C. has it removed one morning before daybreak.

December 1985
The P.P. community planning group presents their plan to the chancellor. The chancellor calls for a hiatus of the planning process after calling this three-year work unacceptable.

Mid 80's
UC begins denying all amplified events in the Park. For almost one and a half years there are no concerts.

18th Anniversary
P.P.C. files a lawsuit in superior court to restrain UC from denying First Amendment activities in the Park.

1987
UC includes People's Park in its long range planning

process.

April 16, 1987

Judge rules in favor of the P.P.C. and a permanent leave injunction is ordered against UC.

1989

UC includes People's Park Council organizers in their first plan of a street fair for the 20th anniversary celebration.

1989

After the civil uprising of May 19th, Alameda County Sheriff Plummer makes public statements and sends a letter to the mayor saying that People's Park issues must be resolved through peaceful means because the county can not afford to mobilize aid every time a Park "riot" occurred and they will continue until some acceptable resolution is reached.

May 19, 1989

Park activists organize a film showing and torchlight march as a memorial to commemorate the murder of James Rector. A bonfire planned to be in front of the building where Rector was shot is ignited prematurely at the intersection of Dwight Way and Telegraph. A large crowd gathers. Police and fire units arrive and put out the fire after some resistance by the protesters. A second fire is is started after the fire and police units leave. When the units return they are not in a playful mood. The firemen open up on the crowd with a powerful water cannon, knocking many off their feet and spraying hot embers into people's faces. This sets the stage for the civil uprising that follows. After the smoke has cleared, two Berkeley fire chief cars are overturned. One is burned. Twenty-eight stores are vandalized and or looted and a quarter of a million dollars worth of damage sustained. Five activists are arrested and first charged with five felony counts. This is later dropped to four misdemeanor counts of inciting a riot, participating in a riot, interfering with firemen, and vandalism.

Throughout the 80's

Park workers install many redwood benches and also build a river-rock water fountain. Community gardens continue to sprout food and flowers. UC continues to develop all of the user-developed Park assets. People's Park Council prepares to sue UC settlers by ordering the UC PD to pay for the damage to the benches.

Spring 1990

Mayor Loni Hancock and chancellor ignore Sheriff Plummer's warnings and have their own private discussions. Together they come up with the document of agreement that leads to the lease that signs People's Park back over to UC.

May 19, 1990

Direct action groups form alliances to demonstrate the activists opposition to the City's role in helping UC reclaim the Park. The city calls in five mutual aid police departments. They rampage southside, chasing down and clubbing protesters. Several activists are seriously injured and many bystanders roughed up. Protesters refrain from retaliating with the exception of graffiti on Mayor Hancock's house and Assemblyman Tom Bates' state car.

July 1990

The city sweeps homeless campers off sidewalks next to the Park. This is part of the mayor's "personal and political" arrangement with UC which forces homeless out southside. UC donates rocks and ground cover to fill in the spaces previously occupied by by the homeless. People's Park Council gardeners assist UC in this effort. UC cuts down a mature tree and uses heavy equipment to clear out "overgrowth" on East End.

Same Period

A People's Park and homeless rights activist is arrested, sent to Santa Rita and held in waist chains for three days for conducting a silent vigil and fast in People's Park in honor of Mitch Snyder, a national homeless rights activist found dead, having hanged himself in the Washington D.C. shelter he fought to establish and save. An earlier public candlelight vigil in the Park is broken up by UC police who enforce the new rule against sleeping in the park, saying the "Park is closed at 10PM".

April 28, 1991
'Yuppification of Southside' —*Slingshot*

"It is obvious that the issue is more than just the Free Box or the Park. It's part of the larger issue of yuppification of Southside and control over People's Park. The

University wants to make the Southside inhospitable to the homeless. People should be ready for a call to protect the park."

May 15, 1991
'People's Park Lease Under Fire' —*Daily Cal*

"Lambasting the People's Park lease as 'laughable,' the Berkeley Parks and Recreation Commission convened Monday evening to discuss site development ideas for the city's portions of the park... The primary concern of the park representatives in attendance seemed to be the size, number and placement of the university-proposed volleyball courts in the grassy middle portion of People's Park that remains under university jurisdiction."

Fall 1991
'City Council Complicity in People's Park Construction' —*Slingshot*

"Many people question why the People's Park supporters have ventured outside the legal system to stop the University's invasion of their land. The truth is the People's Park activists have tried working "in the system" for years and found that the system did not want to hear from them."

Fall 1991
California People's Park Pullout Section —*Slingshot*

New Police Tactics: "Over the past few weeks, demonstrations concerning the fate of People's Park have received considerable public attention. Unknown to most observers of these events, however, are details of new police tactics, UC police in particular, introduced during the latest Free Speech clashes."

How Much does it Cost to Throw a Beach Party in People's Park?: "As the first volleyball games begin, the total cost of the police presence in People's Park continues to mount. Although the University budget for what has been called "the world's most expensive kitty litter box" is $150,000 a year for the next two years, reimbursing Bay Area police department could add an additional $200,00 to the University's costs."

Homeless in Berkeley: "People's Park is not a comprehensive solution to homelessness. But since homelessness is not about to be solved, the Park offers the best hope many of the Berkeley's homeless have. It provides access to food, running water and occasional medical care. Just as important, it is a place to spend time during the day and a place to be at night."

People's Park: A Recent Chronology: A History of People's Park from July 27 - Aug. 4 '91.

A Struggle for the Land: This is a fight over who has the rightful claim to People's Park. "the People": the unincorporated association of People's Park users and the Regents - a small group of white men. This article also includes the story of People's Park, starting in the 60s when it was a block of low income housing. It also questions "property" and ownership and why and how the Regents claim ownership as well as what "the People" claim, referring to the English Common Law.

Enemys of the Park: a cast of characters: A description of the people both in the University and City who are against People's Park being for the people. It states who they are and what they have done against People's Park self-development.

Fall 1991
'Cool Places to Hang Out' —*Slingshot*

"People's park. Contrary to University propaganda, the park is a nice place to hang out."

A little description of People's Park, where and what it is and why it is a nice place to hang out.

Fall 1991
'People's History of Berkeley' —*Slingshot*

"People's Park had two huge struggles in as many quarters and little to show for them. Students and people in Berkeley were frustrated and fought extra hard during the creation of this park."

"The site that is now People's Park was a dirt parking lot at the start of '69. The university had bought the property for new dorms. When it sat empty for some time and became an eyesore, community members decided to build a park on it..."

September 6, 1991
People's Park Annex

A group of people began to build another park on a Telegraph Avenue lot left vacant for years after a fire had destroyed the old Berkeley Inn. Calling it People's Park

Annex, a random group came in with wheelbarrows, shovels and donated plants, and began to transform the lot much as had been done in 1968 and 1969. Some were students, some activists, many were homeless and not by choice. There was little left of the hippie movement- people who slept in the annex on bedrolls, under ragged tents, or on the hard ground, were jobless, hopeless and starving.

When tents went up it looked like the Hooversviles of the 30s, or the California of the Grapes of Wrath. Sadly, the energy that had transformed a vacant lot into a place of hope soon developed other problems. The most serious was lack of sanitary facilities. People who were sick urinated and defecated on the ground. A few hard drug pushers made it rough for everyone. On Nov. 6 at five AM the city moved in and closed the Annex on the grounds that it was a health hazard. Demonstrations were minor. After a few months someone broke through the fence and people's guerrilla art began to appear mysteriously, particularly a group of continuously changing toilet seats which the street artist Richard List called "plop art."

October 1991
The Attack on Public Space (Love and Rage)

"In defiance of the largest, and most violent police deployment in 20 years, hundreds of protesters took to the streets nightly to resist the University of California at Berkeley's attempt to build volleyball courts on the historic People's Park."

By Aug. 5, the police were being forced to de-escalate their forces, due to mounting political opposition and skyrocketing costs."

1992
'People's Park Marchers Protest Slaying'
—S.F. Chronicle

"About 150 demonstrators marched from People's Park to the chancellor's mansion at the University of California at Berkeley yesterday to protest the slaying of an armed intruder last week, breaking windows on several campus buildings and setting small fires along the way."

"The demonstrators, who rallied for two hours at next to People's Park before marching to the UC campus, were angered by the death of Rosebud Abigail Denovo, 19, who was fatally shot Tuesday by an Oakland police officer investigating an early morning break-in at the Chancellor's home."

January 11, 1992
'Violence at People's Park' *—S.F. Examiner*

"Early Friday Berkeley city officials..."

"Court documents filed by attorneys for the Regents cited four members of the Defense Union with allegedly committing various destructive acts at the park. They were Carol Ruth Denney, David Nadel, Robert E Sparks and Michael Lee.

"These people are clearly non-violent. One of the charges is throwing roses into the volleyball court and dancing with a cardboard saw."

February 13, 1992
'Parks and Rec Had Another Plan for Park'
—Berkeley Voice

"Contrary to action taken by the City Council Tuesday, the Parks and Recreation Commission voted Monday night to recommend that the council reconsider the location of the basketball court to be built in People's Park."

The Parks and Recreation department asks that the basketball courts be smaller and placed in the same place as the Volleyball courts. The City agrees to the smaller size but will not agree to put the volleyball and basketball courts in the same area.

March 10, 1992
'24 Arrested at People's Park Protest' —*SF Examiner*

"Berkeley police arrested 24 people yesterday during a noisy demonstration at People's Park where demonstrators tried to prevent workers from starting construction on a basketball court."

A force of 60 officers in riot gear swept more than 100 angry park protesters from the site and the construction crews began their work mid afternoon."

March 12, 1992
'Students Decline to Join Park Battle' —*Berkeley Voice*

"Where have all the students gone? Anywhere but People's Park."

The recent protests to save People's Park have drawn only a couple of students. Most students didn't seem to care much about the park or about understanding why the struggle was important. Some people believe the students fear being punished or harassed by campus officials and don't believe the protesters could win the battle. Most students didn't feel it was a major issue and felt there was too much fuss over a 'small patch of land.'"

April 30, 1992

'Park Activist Wins Council Support' —*The Daily Cal*

"Backed by an army of about 50 raucous supporters, People's Park activist and Ashkenaz Cafe owner David Nadel won unanimous support from the City Council Tuesday night in a suit brought against him by UC Berkeley."

"On Jan. 10 '92 the university charged that Nadel and three other park activists were primary actors in damages to university property in the park. The charges include vandalizing the volleyball courts, moving a portable toilet and assaulting a university employee."

January 13, 1993

'Politically Correct Paving Sought' —*SF Examiner*

"They have invented Indigenous People's Day and championed such causes as saving the ozone layer; now officials of the City of Berkeley are in search of the ultimate liberal statement: the politically correct basketball court."

UC Berkeley is looking to resurface the packed gravel basketball court. The city is looking for an all-natural, non-toxic alternative to good old asphalt. Many people said they would protest the resurfacing of the basketball courts no matter what they used."

March 15, 1993

'People's Park's New Look, Old Woes' —*SF Chronicle*

"After nearly 18 months of painstaking and often controversial renovations, crews have finally completed major construction on Berkeley's People's Park."

"During the past year and a half construction crews have installed sand volleyball courts, a children's play area, a large bathroom, a paved basketball court, new walkways and security lighting - all in an attempt to improve the area's image, encourage more student and community members to use the park and drive out drug dealers who have set up shop in the landmark of Berkeley's counter-culture."

April 23, 1993
'Berkeley Loses Suit to Park Protester'
—Oakland Tribune

"The city of Berkeley has settled a federal court lawsuit with a people's park protester for $18,000 and civil rights attorneys said the city and UC Berkeley face damages from a number of similar suits."

Mitja Che Baumhackl was arrested on Aug.1 1991, the second day of rioting over the volleyball courts. Four police officers cited him for disturbing the peace and confiscated his sign that had obscene suggestions about the University of California, Berkeley. The district attorney did not file charges and Baumhackl sued.

May 2, 1993
'People's Park 'Sacred' at 24' *—Oakland Tribune*

"Hundreds of people packed People's Park to celebrate the 24th anniversary Saturday with music dance skits and speeches that focused on the parks legendary struggle."

This day was also dedicated to Cesar Chavez, who died a week ago. It also celebrated May 1, the International Day of the Working Class. The event epitomized the constant struggle against police brutality. At the People's Park Annex, a UC Berkeley student group called Using Our Education to Rebuild America painted a mural, "unity and harmony to celebrate the day."

May 12, 1993
'Accord on How to Handle Homeless'
—Oakland Tribune

In a precedent-setting agreement with homeless advocates, the city of Oakland, Caltrans and the state police have agreed to new rules about how to handle homeless people and their belongings". The agreement which is waiting to be approved by the federal judge, is the first of its kind to address the question of homeless people's rights and property. The agreement, among other things, states that California Department of Transportation must give 48 hours notice to homeless people encamped on its property. It also states that the police and Caltrans must allow homeless people to gather their things and if that is not possible, Caltrans and the police are not allowed to throw their things away. The city also agreed to pay 13,000 dollars in compensation to seven homeless men and women for the March 1992 sweeps.

July 19, 1993
'Berkeley Sees Profits in its Wacky Image'
—S.F. Examiner

Chunks of officially licensed People's Park sod, tear gas-scented cologne, nuclear-free-zone refrigerator magnets - the merchandising possibilities are endless."

Councilwoman Carla Woodworth put forward the idea that Berkeley could cash on its "wacky counterculture image." By selling souvenirs the city could earn some money. This store that Woodworth thought could bring in about 100,000 dollars a year would sell such souvenirs as: People's Park signs, nuclear-free zone signs, "Naked guy" suntan lotion etc.

December 18, 1993
'People's Potty Stays Open' —*Oakland Tribune*

"The bathroom built at People's Park by the City of Berkeley last year over vociferous protests by park activists has places the city in a catch 22 situation."

The city of Berkeley was caught in a catch 22 after opening the new bathroom in People's Park. The bathroom was put in because neighbors complained that homeless people were going to the bathroom in their yard or in doorways. However the city found that if they kept the bathroom open 24 hours it became an area used for drug trafficking. To solve the problem the city hired a security guard from 10pm - 6am to patrol the area.

May 2, 1994
'Park Gets People Dancing' —*Oakland Tribune*

"It was a day for dancing and nostalgia at People's Park Sunday as a crowd estimated at at least 1,000 commemorated the park's 25th anniversary."

About 1,000 people came out to celebrate the parks 25 anniversary, all kinds of bands and political speeches came out in celebration. The celebration was one of happiness and no problems were reported, the police stated that it was very peaceful.

May 14, 1995
'People's Park Homeless Win Suit'
—Oakland Tribune

"A lawsuit that began after UC Berkeley police and groundskeepers swept up and disposed of debris and personal belongings stored in People's Park in 1990 has ended in a $6,080 judgment."

12 people will be awarded 80 - 1,120 dollars per person to compensate for their personal belongings that were swept up by UC Berkeley police and groundskeepers and destroyed. The 12   homeless people were encamped in people's park at the time. The decision was made after a 3 month Superior Court trial that ended in a 6,080 dollar judgment.

November 9, 1995
'Site Out for Sand Court at Berkeley's People's Park'
—Oakland Tribune

"A long-disputed volleyball court at People's Park, which sparked a week of rioting when it was built by University of California, Berkeley in 1991, is headed for the scrap heap of history."

"A plan to replace the sand court with grass will be presented to the Berkeley City Council Nov.28, a university official said Wednesday." However, the UC is talking about using that grassy area as a sports field 5 or 6 nights a week. Also talked about at the City Council is moving the Catholic volunteers who serve breakfast at the park, into the basement of the Lutheran Church."

November 15, 1995
'People's Park No Longer Haven for Heavy Drinkers'
—Oakland Tribune

"Those with a hankering for a beer in the sun at People's Park better watch out: That whiskery guy sitting nearby maybe an undercover cop."

The Berkeley police have gone undercover at People's Park to crack down on drinking and intoxication. Seven Berkeley officers from the University of California, Berkeley issued 475 citations in people's park - 425 for alcohol-related offenses, in a 10 week period. The police believe their is a connection between petty crime, problems around Telegraph and drinking. Some of the locals, however, felt that the police should be centering their attention on the drug dealers in the park and not so much on the drinking.

November 1995
'Defending the Rights of the Poor in People's Park'
—Street Spirit

"The history of People's Park is a history of struggle for freedom of speech."

"At present, the City of Berkeley and the University of California seem to be trying to drive homeless people away by not including social services in the Park Use plan, ...Members of the community should stand up and fight back for the tradition of providing food and clothing to those who have nothing..."

4-29-96
'People's Park: Celebrating Brighter Future'
—Oakland Tribune

"People's Park - Berkeley's often cursed but much revered monument to the 1960's - was packed Sunday as supporters optimistically celebrated its 27th anniversary with political speeches and live music from a string of bands."

Sunday the park was filled with people celebrating the Park's 27th anniversary with political speeches and live music. The Berkeley city council last week approved a far-reaching deal with park landowner - the University of California - allowing the city to run the park from now on and guaranteeing steady university funding. An 18 member committee has been working on the plan for 4 1/2 years. An informal committee has spent 2 1/2 months interviewing representatives of every conceivable park interest group. The committee found that most people blame the clothing box for the park's unsavory reputation including drug and alcohol use among those hanging out in the area.

July 12, 1996
'Children of Paradise: A Jungian View of People's Park'
—East Bay Express

The night before he was to help lead a workshop called "Awakening the Unconscious at People's Park," Qire Ching dreamed that a man had unleashed a wild dog inside the park."

A People's Park two day workshop is held to "understand" what People's Park means and why it is so important and worth dying for. UC Berkeley representative, city council, FNB's, activists, police, "the Hate Man", homeless people - all different types of people came together to try understand People's Park.

July 12, 1996
'Drumming up an Understanding of People's Park'

"Berkeley - a hundred years from now, People's Park may or may not be a sacred place."

"...Berkeley Ecumenical Chaplaincy for the Homeless has hired an internationally known team of Jungian psychologists who specialize in conflict resolution to hold a workshop. They have invited 130 people from every level of society."

Park: Beset by Old Problems: University ceded control of much of the land to the city as part of a compromise to retain the area as open space. but the lease expires in 1996."

"Buffington said Wednesday the university has agreed to advance the Lutheran chapel the estimated 20,000 dollars it will cost to make the basement wheelchair-accessible..." But FNB's and other groups say they don't want to be in the basement of the Lutheran chapel - they would rather eat outside in the park.

January 11, 1997
'People's Park Activists Victorious' —*Slingshot*

"On Jan. 11, 1997 the University of California at Berkeley put down sod over the hole that once contained the world famous yet seldom used volleyball courts."

January 16, 1997
'David Nadel Remembered' —*Berkeley Voice*

"David Nadel risked everything for his ideals throughout his life, and on Dec.17, 1996 he may have made the ultimate sacrifice."

On Dec. 17, 1996, David Nadel was shot in the head at his club called Ashkenaz. He died two days later in the hospital. David Nadel, originally from Southern California, enjoyed music and especially loved folk dancing. He was a friend to many people and a passionate proponent of assorted ethnic forms of musical expression.

February 1997
'Farewell, David Nadel' —*Street Spirit*

"Every New Year's Eve for the past 23 years, there has been a large reunion of folk dancers at Ashkenaz, the Berkeley club founded by David Nadel and a number of fellow folk dancers in 1973."

On Dec.19, a young man started a disturbance at the Ashkenaz club. David asked him to leave and called the cops - the man left and returned a second time threatening to get a gun and kill David. The cops spoke to the man but did not arrest him or take him away from the area. Later that night the man returned and knocked on the door, when David opened it, the man shot him in the head. David was a strong activist and fought to the bitter end for user development in People's Park.

EPILOGUE

(From the writing of James Agee)

"*While they are still drawn together within the shelter around the center of their parents, these children and their parents together compose a family.*

This family must take care of itself. It has no mother or father. There is no other shelter, nor resource, nor any lover, interest, sustaining strength or comfort, so near, nor can anything happy or sorrowful that comes to anyone in this family possibly mean to those outside it what it means to those within it. But it is, as I have told, inconceivably lonely, drawn upon itself as tramps are drawn around a fire in the cruelest weather and thus in such loneliness it exists among other families each of which is no less lonely, nor any less without help or comfort, and is likewise drawn in upon itself.

Such a family lasts, for a while. The children are held to a magnetic center.

Then in time the magnetism weakens, both of itself in its tiredness of aging and sorrow, and against the strength of the growth of each child, and against the strength of pulls from outside, and one by one the children are drawn away."